The
Anne Boleyn
Collection III

The
Anne Boleyn Collection III
Celebrating Ten Years of TheAnneBoleynFiles

Copyright © 2019
MadeGlobal Publishing

ISBN-13: 978-84-948539-9-9

M
MadeGlobal Publishing

For more information on
MadeGlobal Publishing, visit our website:
www.madeglobal.com

Contents

Dedications

"Le temps viendra, Je Anne Boleyn"

To Queen Anne Boleyn (c.1501-1536) who serves
as my inspiration each and every day.

To my gorgeous family: Tim, Christian, Kira, Iden,
Verity & Joel, with love always.

To my cats and dogs: Boni, Judd, Pippa, Maj,
Ari and Oreo, for the cameos in my daily videos
and for blessing and enriching my life.

To Fern Nissenbaum, who won the
Anne Boleyn Files 10 year Anniversary Competition
– thank you for your support and encouragement.

And to all Tudor history lovers
worldwide – keep "Tudoring"!

Introduction

In 2012, I published my very first book. It was called *The Anne Boleyn Collection* and was a celebration of three years of the Anne Boleyn Files website. It was simply a collection of my most popular blog posts, and I had no idea that it would sell well over 100,000 copies – wow! It was wonderful to know that there were that many people who were not only interested in Anne Boleyn and Tudor history, but who were also interested in what I had to say about it.

My style isn't everyone's cup of tea, and this book is a collection of articles and talks I've done over the last few years, rather than a flowing history book or biography – fair warning! I just want you to know what you're letting yourself in for. It means that there will be a little bit of repetition, and you may also find it rather informal in style.

I like to "talk Tudor" and share my research and thoughts, and I love interacting with my readers and viewers, so please do come and find me and have a chat using the links below.

Thank you for your support,

Claire

https://www.youtube.com/AnneBoleynFiles/
https://www.theanneboleynfiles.com/
https://www.tudorsociety.com/
https://www.facebook.com/theanneboleynfiles/
https://www.facebook.com/tudorsociety/
https://twitter.com/AnneBoleynFiles/
https://twitter.com/thetudorsociety/
https://www.instagram.com/tudor.society/
https://www.instagram.com/anneboleynfiles/

What did Anne Boleyn look like?

In his 1585 book, Rise of the Anglican Schism, Catholic recusant Nicholas Sander described Anne Boleyn:

> "Anne Boleyn was rather tall of stature, with black hair, and an oval face of a sallow complexion as if troubled with jaundice. She had a projecting tooth under the upper lip, and on her right hand six fingers. There was a large wen under her chin, and therefore to hide its ugliness she wore a high dress covering her throat. In this she was followed by the ladies of the court, who also wore high dresses, having before been in the habit of leaving their necks and the upper portion of their persons uncovered. She was handsome to look at, with a pretty mouth, amusing in her ways, playing well on the lute, and was a good dancer."

As I noted in an article on the Anne Boleyn Files, it sounds like Sander was describing Nanny McPhee rather than the woman who caught the eye of King Henry VIII, who he pursued and bombarded with love letters, and who was the catalyst for the break with Rome. However, we can dismiss Sander's description of Anne Boleyn for the following reasons:

- He was writing nearly 50 years after her death
- He was still a child when she died
- There's no evidence that he ever even saw her
- He was a Catholic recusant writing Catholic propaganda in the reign of the Protestant Elizabeth I
- He was against Protestantism which had taken hold in England as a result of Henry VIII breaking with Rome
- He was hostile to Elizabeth I, Henry VIII and Anne Boleyn
- His description is not corroborated by others.

Sander was biased. His purpose was to blacken Elizabeth's name and that of her mother, who he blamed for what happened.

I think it's likely that Sander was inspired by a hostile account of Anne's coronation in 1533 which was once in a catalogue of papers at Brussels. The anonymous writer stated:

> "Her dress was covered with tongues pierced with nails, to show the treatment which those who spoke against her might expect. Her car was so low that the ears of the last mule appeared to those who stood behind to belong to her. The letters H. A. were painted in several places, for Henry and Anne, but were laughed at by many. The crown became her very ill, and a wart disfigured her very much. She wore a violet velvet mantle, with a high ruff (goulgiel) of gold thread and pearls, which concealed a swelling she has, resembling goître."

This is the only contemporary account of Anne having a wart or a goitre, but, as Professor Eric Ives points out in his biography of Anne, Anne's coronation garb would have covered her neck anyway if it was like the surcoat and mantle that Elizabeth I wore at her coronation. Chronicler Edward Hall described Anne as wearing a surcoat of white cloth of gold, a mantle of the same cloth, but trimmed with ermine, and a coif with a circlet of "rich stones". He made no mention of a dress covered with pierced tongues or a particularly high neck. How could this anonymous observer see this wart or goitre anyway? Although I often see this hostile description being attributed to Eustace Chapuys, the imperial ambassador, he did not write it. This account is by an unknown author. Chapuys' account of the coronation processions and pageants is not a glowing one – he compares the pageant to a funeral and describes it as "a cold, poor, and most unpleasing sight" – but he certainly does not give Anne a wen or a wart. The Brussels account is not corroborated by any other contemporary account of Anne's coronation, and as for Sander's mention of Anne making high necks fashionable at court, that simply isn't true. High necks came later. In the 1530s, when Anne was queen, low square necklines were in fashion. Anne's chest and neck would have been on display, and a swelling could not have been hidden by a necklace such as the B necklace that she's often depicted wearing.

I think we can safely rule out the idea that Anne had a projecting tooth, a wen, and an extra finger, but what *did* she look like?

Let's examine some contemporary descriptions...

Lancelot de Carles, secretary to the French ambassador, who was a court when Anne was queen, wrote a poem about Anne and in it he said:

> "She was beautiful and her figure was elegant,
> And her eyes were even more enticing,
> She knew how to use them as is due,
> Sometimes keeping them at rest,
> Other times sending a message
> To convey her heart's secret expression;
> And, without doubt, such was their power
> Which forced many to defer to her."

She was described in February 1528 by a Venetian repeating "advices from France" as "very beautiful".

In a conversation with John Barlowe, Dean of Westbury, recorded by Helwighen of the Emperor's council of Brabant,

Barlowe was asked how Anne Boleyn compared to Elizabeth Blount, the king's earlier mistress:

> "After this I asked him whether he knew personally the girl by whom the King had had his son, and this present lady who, he said, was so much in favour with the King; whether they were pretty or handsome, and whether they were worthy of the King falling in love with them and abandoning his own wife.
>
> The Dean answered that he knew both the lady and the girl; the latter (he said) was prettier than the lady, but this one was more eloquent and graceful, more really handsome, and especially of a good family."

The report was written in French and the original French for Anne's looks was "competement belle", i.e. competently beautiful, beautiful enough.

Theologian Simon Grynée of Basle, in a letter to reformer Martin Bucer, described Anne as "young, good-looking, of a rather dark complexion", and in October 1532, in his summary of the interview between Henry VIII and Francis I in 1532 at Calais, Venetian diplomat Francesco Sanuto said of Anne:

> "Madam Anne is not one of the handsomest women in the world; she is of middling stature, swarthy complexion, long neck, wide mouth, bosom not much raised, and in fact has nothing but the English King's great appetite, and her eyes, which are black and beautiful, and take great effect on those who served the Queen when she was on the throne."

You might think that portraits can help us answer the question "what did Anne Boleyn look like?"

Well, no, not really. As is clear from the multiple portraits we have of the Tudor monarchs and important people, Tudor portraits were more about style and propaganda rather than giving an accurate depiction of the sitter. Then there is the fact that none of the portraits associated with Anne is contemporary. The only contemporary images we have of Anne are the 1534 lead medal (which is damaged in the nose area), a cartoon-like sketch from her coronation banquet seating plan, and possibly an illumination from the 1534 Black Book of the Garter which depicts "The Lady of the Garter". They're not particularly helpful. Stone carver Lucy Churchill did a wonderful job reconstructing and replicating the 1534 medal, but all we can really tell from it is that Anne had a long narrow face.

George Wyatt, the grandson of Thomas Wyatt the Elder, the famous Tudor poet and a man who appears to have been in love with Anne, wrote a treatise defending Anne Boleyn's reputation in the late 16th century. He was obviously not a contemporary of Anne, but I suspect that there were enough people alive around him who knew what Anne looked like and could have corrected his description. Wyatt also states that some of his information came from Anne Gainsford, a lady who served Anne. In his work, Wyatt talks of Anne's "rare and admirable beauty" and goes on to say: "She was taken at that time to have a beauty not so whitely as clear and fresh above all we may esteem, which appeared much more excellent by her favour passing sweet and cheerful" and he also wrote of "small moles incident to the clearest complexions", as well as "some little show of a nail" on the side of one of her fingers.

In 1876, while restoration work was done on the Chapel of St Peter ad Vincula at the Tower of London, the resting place of Anne Boleyn, the chancel floor had to be raised and some of the remains exhumed. In the spot where Anne Boleyn was recorded as being buried, the Victorian team found the remains of a woman and these were examined by Queen Victoria's pathologist. Of the remains, Dr Frederick Mouat stated that they belonged to "a female of between twenty-five and thirty years of age, of a delicate frame of body, and who had been of slender and perfect proportions; the forehead and lower jaw were small and especially well formed. The vertebrae were particularly small, especially one joint (the atlas), which was that next to the skull, and they bore witness to the Queen's 'lyttel neck'"

In a memorandum, he gave further details:

"The bones of the head indicate a well-formed round skull, with an intellectual forehead, straight orbital ridge, large eyes, oval face and rather square full chin. The remains of the vertebrae, and the bones of the lower limbs, indicate a well-formed woman of middle height, with a short and slender neck. The ribs show depth and roundness of chest. The hands and feet bones indicate delicate and well-shaped hands and feet, with tapering fingers and a narrow foot."

In another report, he gave her height at around 5' to 5' 3. Of course, we don't know that these remains definitely belonged to her, but they were where the team expected to find them.

And what about her hair?

Lancelot de Carles describes the infant Princess Elizabeth, Anne and Henry VIII's daughter, in his poem:

"A beautiful child of pure colouring,
Whose looks very much resembled her father's,
Certainly more than her mother's, the Queen:"

So Elizabeth had fair colouring like her father – the Tudor pale skin and golden or red hair. Elizabeth being fair like her father, suggests that Anne was dark-haired. This is corroborated by Thomas Wyatt the Elder, who wrote a poem called "Brunet and Phyllis". We know that Brunet referred to Anne Boleyn because, as Nicola Shulman notes in her biography of Wyatt, he originally wrote:

"If thou ask whom, sure since I did refrain,
Her that did set our country in a roar."

"Brunet" must surely imply that Anne had dark brown hair, particularly as the woman in the poem is contrasted with Phyllis, who was Wyatt's mistress Elizabeth Darrell, who was blonde-haired.

Dark brown/almost black is the hair colour we see in portraits like the Hever Castle painting of Anne holding a red rose, but in the National Portrait Gallery one and the pretty miniature by John Hoskins, Anne has hair that is best described as chestnut. Many women have dark hair with reddish tones. Before my hair started going grey, it was dark brown and would get red highlights in the summer, so perhaps Anne was like that.

Putting the contemporary descriptions together with the 1534 medal and Dr Mouat's report, we have a woman who was of average height for her time with a long oval face, an olive complexion, a long neck, wide mouth, small breasts, with dark eyes and dark hair, and perhaps moles on her skin. Her eyes seem to have had an effect on those around her, and she was elegant.

Although she may not have been as beautiful as some around her and perhaps did not fit the ideals of beauty at the time, there was something about her that attracted Henry Percy, Thomas Wyatt and Henry VIII. When I picture Anne in my head, she's like Genevieve Bujold from Anne of the Thousand Days.

Resources

My video from back in 2011 on "Anne Boleyn's Appearance", which looks at some of the portraits of Anne, can be found at https://youtu.be/jfTI2ffP9j8

Coronation seating plan – see image at https://www. theanneboleynfiles.com/1st-june-1533-the-noble-triumphant-coronation-of-queen-anne-boleyn/

1534 medal - https://www.britishmuseum.org/research/collection_online/collection_object_details/collection_image_gallery.aspx?assetId=216454001&objectId=953013&partId=1

http://www.lucychurchill.com/AnneBoleynMedal.php

https://tudorfaces.blogspot.com/2017/04/anne-boleyn-as-lady-of-garter.html

Notes and Sources

Sander, Nicholas (1585), translated by David Lewis (1877) *Rise and Growth of the Anglican Schism, Burns and Oates.*

de Carles, Lancelot, "Poème sur la Mort d'Anne Boleyn", in La Grande Bretagne devant L'Opinion Française depuis la Guerre de Cent Ans jusqu'a la Fin du XVI Siècle, Georges Ascoli.

'Henry VIII: June 1533, 1-5', in Letters and Papers, Foreign and Domestic, Henry VIII, Volume 6, 1533, ed. James Gairdner (London, 1882), pp. 262-275. British History Online http://www.british-history.ac.uk/letters-papers-hen8/vol6/pp262-275

'Spain: June 1533, 1-25', in Calendar of State Papers, Spain, Volume 4 Part 2, 1531-1533, ed. Pascual de Gayangos (London, 1882), pp. 703-715. British History Online http://www.british-history.ac.uk/cal-state-papers/spain/vol4/no2/pp703-715

'Venice: February 1528', in Calendar of State Papers Relating To English Affairs in the Archives of Venice, Volume 4, 1527-1533, ed. Rawdon Brown (London, 1871), pp. 118-125. British History Online http://www.british-history.ac.uk/cal-state-papers/venice/vol4/pp118-125

Ives, Eric (2004) *The Life and Death of Anne Boleyn*, Wiley-Blackwell.

'Spain: June 1532, 21-30', in Calendar of State Papers, Spain, Volume 4 Part 2, 1531-1533, ed. Pascual de Gayangos (London, 1882), pp. 462-478. British History Online http://www.british-history.ac.uk/cal-state-papers/spain/vol4/no2/pp462-478

Simon Grynée quoted in Sergeant, P. W. (1923) *The Life of Anne Boleyn*, Hutchinson, p.129.

'Preface', in Calendar of State Papers Relating To English Affairs in the Archives of Venice, Volume 4, 1527-1533, ed. Rawdon Brown (London, 1871), pp. vii-xxxvii. British History

Online http://www.british-history.ac.uk/cal-state-papers/
venice/vol4/vii-xxxvii

Wyatt, George *Extracts from the life of the Virtuous Christian and
Renowned Queen Anne Boleigne,* in Cavendish, George (1827)
The Life of Cardinal Wolsey, Samuel Weller Singer.

Bell, Doyne C. (1877) *Notices of the Historic Persons Buried in
the Chapel of St Peter ad Vincula in the Tower of London, With
an Account of the Discovery of the Supposed Remains of Anne
Boleyn,* John Murray.

Was Anne Boleyn "nice"?

My old English literature teacher would be appalled by that question, not because she had any strong opinion about Anne but because she hated the word "nice" with a vengeance. She viewed it as weak and inadequate, a word that didn't describe anything properly. However, this question is one I get asked on a regular basis and the word "nice" is always used.

According to the Oxford Dictionary, "nice", when used to describe a person, means " good-natured; kind". Can we describe someone we don't know from 500 years ago as "good-natured" or "kind", or even the opposite: "nasty" or "spiteful"?

I don't believe so.

As Professor Eric Ives wrote in his book, *The Life and Death of Anne Boleyn*, even "historians see through a glass darkly; they know in part and they pronounce in part" and "What Anne really was, as distinct from what Anne did, comes over very much less clearly." We can only judge Anne Boleyn from primary sources, but this evidence does not give us a clear picture of her. How can we judge someone's personality on actions and words recorded in documents when we don't know what else they said or did? The Anne of the sources is a conundrum:

"To us she appears inconsistent – religious yet aggressive, calculating yet emotional, with the light touch of the courtier yet the strong grip of the politician – but is this what she was, or merely what we strain to see through the opacity of the evidence? As for her inner life, short of miraculous cache of new material, we shall never really know." (Ives)

In our hunt for the real Anne Boleyn, we are limited by evidence and also by the bias and opinions of those writing that evidence. No description of Anne's personality is objective; it is someone's opinion of her based on their experience of her. You and I might meet the same woman and come away with completely different opinions of her. She may be in a good mood when I meet her but then her mood has changed when you meet her, and she comes across completely differently. I'd describe her as pleasant and good-natured, you'd describe her as moody and unfriendly. Neither of us is right or wrong; we're just making a snap judgement on our limited experience of that woman.

To some, Anne Boleyn is a saint or martyr, to others, she is a whore and bitch, and both points of view can be argued and backed up with evidence. Those who see her as a saint might back up their view with the work of martyrologist John Foxe who viewed Anne as a martyr of the Reformation, a "zealous defender" of the Gospel and a "bountiful" helper of the poor. George Wyatt, grandson of Thomas Wyatt, and William Latymer, Anne's chaplain, also wrote of Anne's generosity and the way she helped those less fortunate than herself. If we relied on those sources alone, we would view Anne as a pious and generous woman who went out of her way to help people. Those who view Anne as a whore and bitch, might back up their view with the letters of Eustace Chapuys, the Imperial ambassador, who referred to Anne Boleyn as "the concubine" and "putain" (whore) and who wrote of Anne stating "that she wished all Spaniards were at the bottom of the sea" and "that she did not care anything for the Queen, and would rather see her hanged than acknowledge her as her mistress." Can one woman be kind and giving, but also spiteful and hot-tempered? Of course she can!

Anne Boleyn was a real person. She is not the product of

fiction, she is not some super-heroine to put on a pedestal, she was a real woman with gifts, talents and positive personality traits, but also character flaws. She accomplished so much, but she also made mistakes. Anne was loving and giving, she stepped in and helped people in dire straits, but she also encouraged the ill-treatment of Catherine of Aragon and Mary. I expect she was fiercely loyal and loving to her family and friends, yet quite probably rejoiced in the fall of those she saw as her enemies. She was human and, like all of us, she was a complex person who showed different sides of her nature to different people.

We like to sort people into goodies and baddies; it's human nature:

- Henry VIII the tyrant versus Henry VIII virtuous prince.
- Jane Seymour the meek and mild versus Jane the plotting woman who stole Henry from Anne and danced on her grave.
- Henry VII the goodie saving England from Richard III the baddie, versus Henry VII the usurper and Richard III the King who was wronged.
- Thomas More the Saint and family man versus the More who delighted in burning reformers.

We even do it with modern day celebrities, politicians and leaders. But people don't fit neatly into little boxes, pigeon holes or labels, do they? Is it so difficult to realise that nobody is all bad or all good? Can't we see that it's impossible to judge people when sources are limited and biased, and we have little or no understanding of the times in which they lived? Goodies and baddies belong in cartoons, not history or real life, and even writers of fiction need to give their characters different facets, otherwise they are not believable.

Eric Ives concluded his biography of Anne Boleyn by writing of the woman he had researched for decades:

"Yet what does come to us across the centuries is the impression of a person who is strangely appealing to the early twenty-first century. A woman in her own right – taken on her own terms in a man's world; a woman who mobilised her education, her style and her presence to outweigh the disadvantages of her sex; of only moderate good looks, but taking a court and a king by storm. Perhaps, in the end, it is Thomas Cromwell's assessment that comes nearest: intelligence, spirit and courage."

That idea of Anne will resonate with many people reading this article, but others will see her differently. What fascinates me about her will be different to what fascinates you, and that's fine, just remember that she wasn't the perfect woman, but she also wasn't the devil incarnate.

Notes and Sources

OxfordDictionaries.com

Ives, Eric. (2005) *The Life and Death of Anne Boleyn,* New ed. Wiley-Blackwell, p.359

Foxe, John. (1851) *Foxe's Book of Martyrs: Acts and Monuments of the Church in Three Volumes*, Vol. II, London, George Virtue

Wyatt, George *The Life of Queen Anne Boleigne* in Cavendish, George. (1825) *The Life of Cardinal Wolsey*, Volume 2. Samuel Weller Singer

ed. Dowling, Maria (1990) *William Latymer's Cronickille of Anne Bulleyne*, Camden Miscellany XXX 39

'Henry VIII: January 1531, 1-15', in Letters and Papers, Foreign and Domestic, Henry VIII, Volume 5, 1531-1532, ed. James Gairdner (London, 1880), pp. 10-22. British History Online http://www.british-history.ac.uk/letters-papers-hen8/vol5/pp10-22 [accessed 18 January 2019

Mary Boleyn and Henry VIII

Whenever I write about Mary Boleyn on the Anne Boleyn Files or mention her on social media, I receive questions about her relationship with the king, for example, when did it start? Why do historians date it to 1522? How long did it last? Were her children fathered by the king? etc. So I thought I would write a brief article looking at the evidence for Mary's relationship with Henry VIII.

Mary Boleyn is a shadowy figure and although she has been the subject of biographies, novels and movies, very little is known about her. Although she is often portrayed as Henry VIII's favourite mistress or the Boleyn woman he really loved, we have no details at all about the king's affair with Mary. We only know that they even had a sexual relationship because the king applied for a dispensation from the Pope in 1527 to enable him to marry her sister, Anne.

In her biography of Mary Boleyn, Alison Weir comments "Henry VIII's affair with Mary Boleyn was conducted so discreetly that there is no record of the date it started, its duration, or when it ended" and she's right. Apart from the dispensation, all we have is gossip and hearsay, most of it resulting from news of the dispensation:

Dr Pedro Ortiz, the imperial ambassador in Rome, wrote

to the Empress in 1533, "that some time ago he [Henry] sent to ask his holiness for a dispensation to marry her, notwithstanding the affinity between them on account of his having committed adultery with her sister."

Charles V, the Holy Roman Emperor, spoke to Dr Richard Sampson, one of Henry VIII's ambassadors, in January 1530 about Henry's quest for an annulment and mentioned that "the said king had kept company with the sister of her whom he now, it was stated, wanted to marry."

Eustace Chapuys, the imperial ambassador in England, wrote that "Even if he could separate from the queen, he could not have her [Anne], for he has had to do with her sister."

Cardinal Pole reproached Henry VIII for sleeping with Mary in his 1538 treatise *pro ecclesiasticae unitatis defensione*, accusing Henry of "seducing her, and then with retaining her as his mistress."

John Hale, Vicar of Isleworth, wrote in 1535 of how a monk at St Bridget's Priory Abbey had pointed out Henry Carey, Mary's son, as being the king's bastard son: "Moreover, Mr. Skydmore dyd show to me yongge Master Care, saying that he was our suffren Lord the Kynge's son by our suffren Lady the Qwyen's syster, whom the Qwyen's grace myght not suffer to be yn the Cowrte".

It appears to have been a known fact that Henry VIII had slept with Anne's sister, but this doesn't help us to date the relationship in any way. Most historians date the relationship to the 1520s, beginning in 1522. This is because at the Shrovetide joust of 2nd March 1522 Henry VIII rode out with the motto *Elle mon Coeur a navera*, or "She has wounded my Heart", embroidered on the trappings of his horse. A woman may have rebuffed the king's advance, or it may simply have been a chivalric theme for the Shrovetide entertainment that year. Even if the theme was based on the king's love-life, we cannot be sure that the woman was Mary, who, by this time, had been married to William Carey for two years. Mary could well have been just a one night stand when

Elizabeth Blount, the king's former mistress, was pregnant with the king's son in 1519. They may not have had a long-lasting affair at all, but the king still needed to declare the impediment whether the relationship had been one night, two nights or many nights.

Evidence that is used to back up the idea that Mary was Henry VIII's mistress from 1522, during her marriage to William Carey, and that one or both of her children were fathered by the king, is the list of grants and offices that Carey was granted between 1522 and his death in 1528. Carey was indeed awarded many lucrative grants and offices, including keeperships and manors, and he also kept his post of Gentleman of the Privy Chamber through Cardinal Wolsey's 1526 purge, the Eltham Ordinances. However, Carey was related to the king and was a royal favourite. Henry Norris, another Gentleman of the Privy Chamber at this time, also survived the Eltham Ordinances, being promoted to Groom of the Stool, and was granted a host of royal grants, keeperships and offices, but nobody suggests that his wife, Mary Fiennes, was sleeping with the king or that his children, born between 1524 and 1526, were the king's bastards.* Henry VIII was generous to those who served him, and William Carey was a loyal servant to him. We can't read too much into these rewards.

We're left with more questions than answers when we delve into the subject of Mary Boleyn's relationship with the king. All we know for certain is that they had a sexual relationship at some point. Although the relationship is always dated to 1522, it could well have taken place earlier, before Mary Boleyn married William Carey. That would make it similar to Henry VIII's relationship with Elizabeth (Bessie) Blount. Bessie was his mistress when she was single, and the king arranged a marriage for her, with Gilbert Tailboys, when he had finished with her. We know that the king attended Mary and Carey's wedding in 1520 so he may well have arranged it.

It is frustrating that so little is known about this Boleyn girl, but she makes the perfect blank canvas for novelists.

Notes and Sources

*Norris' grants included: 1515 – Received his first royal grant, 1518/19 – bailiff of Ewelme, 1519 – Awarded an annuity of 50 marks, 1523 – Granted the keepership of Langley New Park, Buckinghamshire, and was made bailiff of Watlington, 1529 – received a grant of £100 a year from the revenues of the see of Winchester, 1531 – Made chamberlain of North Wales, 1534 – Made Constable of Beaumaris Castle, 1535 – Grants of manors once held by Thomas More, made constable of Wallingford Castle.

Carey's grants included: 1522 – keepership of Beaulieu and bailiff of the manors of New Hall, Walkeford Hall and Powers, 1522 – Wardship and lands of Thomas Sharpe, 1523 – An annuity of 50 marks, 1523 – Receiver and bailiff of Writtle, Keeper of Writtle, 1523 – Constable of Pleshy, 1524 – Made keeper of Wanstead Manor and awarded the grant of several manors in Essex, 1526 – granted several manors in Buckinghamshire, Hampshire and Wiltshire.

Kelly, Henry Ansgar (2004) *The Matrimonial Trials of Henry VIII*, Wipf & Stock Publisher, p.47.

Quoted in Weir, Alison (2011) *Mary Boleyn: The Great and Infamous Whore*, p.30.

Friedmann, Paul G. (1884) (2010) *Anne Boleyn: A Chapter of English History 1527-1536*, Volume II, Macmillan & Co., Appendix, p. 325.

Ellis, Henry (1827) *Original letters, Illustrative of English history*, Volume 2, p.43.

John Hale, Vicar of Isleworth to the Council, 'Henry VIII: April 1535, 11-20', in Letters and Papers, Foreign and Domestic, Henry VIII, Volume 8, January-July 1535, ed. James Gairdner (London, 1885), pp. 202-218. British History Online http://www.british-history.ac.uk/letters-papers-hen8/vol8/pp202-218.

Mary Boleyn, Queen Elizabeth II and the royal family

I'm often asked whether Mary Boleyn, Anne Boleyn's sister, has any living descendants. Yes, is the answer: lots because her children had large families, then their children had large families and so on. What is very interesting about Mary Boleyn's line is that her descendants include today's royal family.

Our present queen, Queen Elizabeth II, descends from Mary Boleyn. Here is the line of descent [Note: each new line is a child of the couple on the previous line, e.g. Catherine Carey was the daughter of Mary Boleyn and William Carey]:

- Mary Boleyn (d. 1543) m. William Carey
- Catherine Carey (c.1524-1569) m. Sir Francis Knollys
- Lettice Knollys (1543-1634) m. Walter Devereux, 1st Earl of Essex
- Robert Devereux, 2nd Earl of Essex (1565-1601) m. Frances Walsingham
- Frances Devereux (1599-1674) m. William Seymour, Duke of Somerset

- Jane Seymour (1637-1679) m. Charles Boyle, 3rd Viscount Dungarvan
- Charles Boyle, 2nd Earl of Burlington (d. 1704) m. Juliana Noel
- Richard Boyle, 3rd Earl of Burlington (1695-1753) m. Dorothy Savile
- Charlotte Elizabeth Boyle (1731-1754) m. William Cavendish, 4th Duke of Devonshire
- Dorothy Cavendish (1750-1794) m. William Cavendish-Bentinck, 3rd Duke of Portland, Prime Minister
- Lieutenant-Colonel Lord Charles Bentinck (1780-1826) m. Anne Wellesley (Lady Abdy)
- Reverend Charles Cavendish-Bentinck (1817-1865) m. Carolina Louis Burnaby
- Cecilia Nina Cavendish-Bentinck (1862-1938) m. Claude Bowes-Lyon, 14th Earl of Strathmore and Kinghorne
- Elizabeth Bowes-Lyon, Queen Elizabeth the Queen Mother (1900-2002) m. King George VI
- Queen Elizabeth II (1926-) m. Prince Philip of Greece and Denmark, now known as Prince Philip, Duke of Edinburgh

Princes William, Duke of Cambridge, and Prince Harry, Duke of Sussex, are descended from Mary Boleyn not only through their father, Prince Charles, who is obviously the son of Queen Elizabeth II, but also through their mother's Spencer family ancestry.

- Mary Boleyn (d. 1543) m. William Carey
- Henry Carey, 1st Baron Hunsdon (1526-1596) m. Anne Morgan
- Robert Carey, 1st Earl of Monmouth (c. 1560-1639) m. Elizabeth Trevannion
- Thomas Carey of Sunninghill Park (d. 1634) m. Margaret Smith

- Elizabeth Carey, Viscountess Mordaunt (1632-1679) m. John Mordaunt, 1st Viscount Mordaunt
- Brigadier-General Lewis Mordaunt (d. 1713) m. Mary Collyer
- Anna Maria Mordaunt (d. 1771) m. Stephen Poyntz
- Margaret Georgiana Poyntz, Countess Spencer (1737-1814) m. John Spencer, 1st Earl Spencer
- George Spencer, 2nd Earl Spencer (1758-1834) m. Lady Lavinia Bingham
- Frederick Spencer, 4th Earl Spencer (1798-1857) m. Adelaide Horatia Seymour
- Charles Spencer, 6th Earl Spencer (1857-1922) m. Hon. Margaret Baring
- Albert Spencer, 7th Earl Spencer (1892-1975) m. Lady Cynthia Hamilton
- John Spencer, 8th Earl Spencer (1924-1992) m. Frances Roche
- Diana, Princess of Wales ((1961-1997) m. Charles, Prince of Wales
- Prince William, Duke of Cambridge (1982-) m. Catherine Middleton, and Prince Harry, Duke of Sussex (1984-) m. Meghan Markle.

At the time of writing this, Prince William has three children: Prince George (b. 2013), Princess Charlotte (b. 2015) and Prince Louis (b. 2018), and Prince Harry and his wife have one child, Archie Harrison (b. 2019). The Boleyn bloodline continues!

I've also been asked whether the Tudor bloodline continues, and it does. Although the Tudor dynasty ended with Elizabeth I in 1603 because she had no children, Henry VIII had two sisters, Margaret and Mary, and their bloodlines continued. Our present queen descends from Margaret Tudor, and therefore King Henry VII:

- Henry VII (1457-1509) m. Elizabeth of York
- Margaret Tudor (1489-1541) m. King James VI of Scotland

- James V of Scotland (1512-1542) m. Mary of Guise
- Mary, Queen of Scots (1542-1587) m. Henry Stuart, Lord Darnley
- James I of England (James VI of Scotland) m. Anne of Denmark
- Elizabeth Stuart, Queen of Bohemia (1596-1662) m. Frederick V, Elector Palatine
- Sophia of Hanover (1630-1714) m. Ernest Augustus, Elector of Hanover
- King George I (1660-1727) m. Sophia Dorothea of Celle
- King George II (1683-1760) m. Caroline of Ansbach
- Frederick, Prince of Wales (1707-1751) m. Princess Augusta of Saxe-Gotha
- King George III (1738-1820) m. Charlotte of Mecklenburg-Strelitz
- Prince Edward, Duke of Kent and Strathearn (1767-1820) m. Princess Victoria of Saxe-Coburg-Saalfeld
- Queen Victoria (1819-1901) m. Prince Albert of Saxe-Coburg and Gotha
- King Edward VII (1841-1910) m. Alexandra of Denmark
- King George V (1865-1936) m. Mary of Teck
- King George VI (1895-1952) m. Elizabeth Bowes-Lyon

Anne Boleyn and Henry Percy

In late 1521, Anne Boleyn was recalled from serving Queen Claude in France. She had been on the Continent since the summer of 1513, when she had joined the court of Margaret of Austria, and moved on to France to serve Mary Tudor, Queen of France, in late 1514, and remained there to serve Queen Claude.

The imperial ambassadors reported to Emperor Charles V in January 1522 that Anne had been called home to England because Cardinal Thomas Wolsey "intended, by her marriage, to pacify certain quarrels and litigation between Boleyn and other English nobles." The Boleyns and St Legers (Thomas Boleyn's aunt's family) were, at this time, arguing with Piers Butler over the title Earl of Ormond, following the death of Thomas Boleyn's grandfather, Thomas Butler, 7th Earl of Ormond. Cardinal Wolsey was attempting to broker a marriage between Piers's son, James, and Thomas Boleyn's daughter, Anne, to put an end to the dispute.

We don't know exactly when Anne arrived back in England, but we know that she was back in time to play the part of Perseverance in the Château Vert pageant. This was held at York Place on 4th March 1522, Shrove Tuesday, as part of the Shrovetide celebrations which also celebrated the negotiations between Charles V, Holy Roman Emperor, and Henry VIII for a joint attack on France.

In Volume 1 of his *The Life of Cardinal Wolsey*, written in the mid-to-late 1550s, George Cavendish, who served as gentleman usher to Cardinal Thomas Wolsey, records how Anne Boleyn returned from France and was admitted to Queen Catherine of Aragon's household, "among whom for her excellent gesture and behaviour, [she] did excel all other; in so much, as the king began to kindle the brand of amours; which was not known to any person, ne scantily to her own person."

The king wasn't the only man who noticed Anne. Cavendish tells of how Henry Percy, a member of Cardinal Wolsey's household and the son and heir of the Earl of Northumberland, who was and would often spend "his pastime" in the Queen's chambers, also fell for Anne and "there grew such a secret love between them that, at length, they were insured together, intending to marry."

According to Cavendish, the king found out about the couple's relationship and was "much offended". Cavendish explains that the king spoke to Wolsey and "consulted with him to infringe the precontract between them". Wolsey called Percy to him and in front of other members of his household, including Cavendish, berated him for his "peevish folly" and reminded him of his status and how he needed the consent of his father and the king for a relationship. Wolsey went on to explain that Percy had offended his father and his king by matching himself with "one, such as neither the king, ne yet your father will be agreeable with the matter." Wolsey explained that he had sent for Percy's father, who would either break off the pre-contract or disinherit his son, and that the king had a match in mind for Anne Boleyn.

Percy is said to have reacted by weeping and apologising. He defended his choice of Anne as a potential wife, by talking of her noble birth, and asked Wolsey to intercede with the king on his behalf. When Wolsey was not willing to do so, Percy then apparently said "but in this matter I have gone so far, before many so worthy witnesses, that I know not how to avoid my self nor to discharge my conscience." However, when Wolsey assured him that it could all be sorted out, Percy agreed to submit to the king and the cardinal.

Percy's father was then called to court. He was furious with his son, saying that he'd always been "a proud, presumptuous, disdainful, and a very unthrift waster". After a good telling off, he departed with some last advice: "see that you do your duty". The mess was then sorted out, and it was arranged for Percy to marry Mary Talbot, daughter of the Earl of Shrewsbury.

Cavendish then tells of the reaction of Anne Boleyn to this news. According to him, she "was greatly offended" and swore revenge on the cardinal, which Cavendish believed to be unfair seeing as Wolsey was only doing the king's bidding.

R W Hoyle, Percy's biographer at Oxford DNB states:

> "According to the cardinal's biographer George Cavendish, Wolsey stopped the courtship because the king had designs on Anne, but the dating makes this impossible. The likely reason for his intervention was the threat to existing plans to marry Percy to Mary Talbot and Anne to James Butler, son of Piers Butler, who was then claiming the earldom of Ormond against Anne's father, Sir Thomas Boleyn. Wolsey summoned Percy's father to court, and he admonished his son sharply for his recklessness. By the end of 1523, the affair was over; Percy married Mary Talbot between 14 January and 8 February 1524."

A pre-contract?

Margaret Schaus, in *Women and Gender in Medieval Europe: An Encyclopedia*, explains that "precontract was the most frequent region alleged for annulment of marriage by the ecclesiastical courts" in the medieval period. Conor McCarthy, in *Marriage in Medieval England: Law, Literature, and Practice*, writes that "a previous contract rendered a subsequent one void" so if a couple had entered a secret marriage or betrothal, i.e. swapped promises, and one of them had gone on to marry again, then this second marriage would be invalid and could be annulled. Of course, in 1483 Richard III had become king after it was alleged that Edward IV had been pre-contracted to Lady Eleanor Butler at the time of his marriage to Elizabeth Woodville. This alleged pre-contract made Edward's marriage to Elizabeth invalid and his children, who included Edward V, illegitimate and therefore out of the line of succession.

According to a letter from Eustace Chapuys, the imperial ambassador, to Charles V in July 1532, Henry Percy had to deny, in front of the king's council, a pre-contract between himself and Anne Boleyn. This was after his wife, Mary Talbot, had reported that Percy had told her in a quarrel that he was not really her husband because he had previously been betrothed, or legally contracted, to Anne. Mary Talbot had written of the quarrel and alleged pre-contract in a letter to her father, the Earl of Shrewsbury, asking him to tell the king, but, instead, the Duke of Norfolk was informed of the matter, and he told his niece, Anne Boleyn. Anne boldly decided that it was best to confront Henry VIII with the matter and ask him to investigate it. Percy was interrogated and denied the pre-contract by swearing an oath on the Blessed Sacrament, in front of Norfolk, the archbishops and the king's canon lawyers. Anne Boleyn also denied the pre-contract.

In May 1536, after Anne Boleyn's arrest, Percy denied the pre-contract once again. It appears that he had been approached in the hope that he would admit to there being a pre-contract between himself and Anne Boleyn, thus providing grounds for an annulment of the king's marriage to Anne. Thomas Cromwell had sent Sir Reynold Carnaby to exert some pressure on Henry Percy. Carnaby was a king's officer in the north of England, and someone Percy knew well, but Percy refused to be bullied into confessing. He stuck to his story: there was no pre-contract.

It is impossible to know what happened between Henry

Percy and Anne Boleyn. Cavendish refers to a "precontract" and writes of how Percy said that he had "gone so far, before many so worthy witnesses", but it is unlikely that he was privy to all Wolsey's conversations with the young man and he was writing his biography thirty years after the events. Wolsey doesn't seem to have had any qualms about sorting the situation out and helping marry Percy off to Mary Talbot, and then later helping the king with his quest to annul his first marriage so that he could marry Anne Boleyn. Something that has made me doubt the veracity of Cavendish's account is his insistence that the cardinal broke up the romance because of the king's interest in Anne Boleyn. We don't have any firm evidence of the king's interest in Anne until 1526/7, around three or four years later.

Was Anne punished?

Cavendish writes of how Percy was "commanded to avoid her company" and that Anne was "commanded to avoid the court and sent home again to her father for a season; whereat she smoked: for all this while she knew nothing of the king's intended purpose." However, we don't know how long she stayed at Hever Castle, the Boleyn family home in the Kent countryside, and when she returned to court, or even if Cavendish's account is even true.

We also don't know Anne's feelings on the matter of her romance with Percy being broken up. Was her heart broken? Had it been true love? We don't know, but if Cavendish's account is true then Percy wept over it, and Anne vowed to take revenge on the cardinal. Cavendish was, of course, writing from hindsight. He was writing long after the fall of his beloved master and then the subsequent fall of Anne Boleyn, so perhaps this coloured his views and we don't know how he heard of Anne's reaction. It's certainly not enough evidence to blame Wolsey's fall in 1530 on Anne Boleyn. The late historian Eric Ives wrote in his biography of Anne: "To go about making threats against the cardinal in 1522 or 1523 was both unwise and childish, and

Anne was neither. When we have some first-hand evidence of her relationship with Wolsey some six or seven years later, it is far more subtle than is explicable by a long-held grudge." And David Loades notes: "Anne had no incentive to undermine Wolsey's position with the King as long as he seemed to be the most likely person to secure the annulment of Henry's marriage."

Whatever her feelings regarding Henry Percy, it must have been humiliating and disappointing to have been sent home to Hever, when she'd spent the last few years at the dazzling French court and had only just arrived at the English one. Was there gossip about her and Percy? If Percy's father came to court and tore strips off his son, and if Anne was ordered home to Hever, then there surely must have been quite a few tongues wagging. Heartache and scandal, not a great way to make a debut at the English court.

Henry Percy was forced to marry Mary Talbot and it appears to have been an unhappy marriage. R.W. Hoyle, in Percy's Oxford Dictionary of National Biography entry, states that the couple were living apart from around late 1529, following the birth of a stillborn child in the April. Hoyle comments that although it is uncertain just how far Percy's relationship with Anne went, "There was nothing uncertain about the earl's relationship with his wife, however: Northumberland clearly loathed her and took pleasure in leaving her unprovided for at his death." The Earl suffered from ill-health, thinking he was dying in 1529 from his "old disease", and he had further bouts of illness between 1532 and 1534. It is reported that he collapsed in May 1536 at Anne Boleyn's trial, after finding her "guilty" as one of the peers chosen to judge her. He died on 29 June 1537, just over a year after Anne, at Hackney, where he was buried in the parish church. He died a natural death, his ill-health preventing him from becoming tangled up in the Pilgrimage of Grace rebellion like his brothers.

His story seems such a sad one: a love affair broken up, an unhappy marriage, the loss of a child, a separation, seeing the woman he loved marrying the king, having to sit in judgement on Anne and then knowing that the judgement led to her execution, suffering from regular bouts of illness, seeing one brother executed and the other imprisoned, and then dying at the age of about 35. But although he had to sit in judgement on Anne, he did not ever change his story about their relationship and the alleged pre-contract. The truth about their relationship died with them.

Notes and Sources

Cavendish, George (1825) *The Life of Cardinal Wolsey, Vol 1*, pp. 57-66.

Friedmann, Paul. *Anne Boleyn: A Chapter of English History 1527-1536, Volume I,* pp.160-61. Friedmann cites Chapuys' letter 1532 from Vienna Archives. Eric Ives, in his notes for p.166 of his book *The Life and Death of Anne Boleyn* gives the reference for Chapuys' letter as Vienna, Haus-, Hof- und Staatsarchiv, England Korrespondenz Karton 5, Konvolut 1532, ff. 81-2.

Hoyle, R. W.. "Percy, Henry Algernon, sixth earl of Northumberland (c.1502–1537)." R. W. Hoyle In Oxford Dictionary of National Biography, edited by H. C. G. Matthew and Brian Harrison. Oxford: OUP, 2004.

Ives, Eric (2004) *The Life and Death of Anne Boleyn*, Blackwell Publishing, pp. 65, 67.

Loades, David (2009) *The Six Wives of Henry VIII*, Amberley Publishing, p. 51.

Did Henry VIII love Anne Boleyn?

This article is based on the first of a series of videos I recorded answering questions that I had received on the Anne Boleyn Files website about Anne Boleyn.

"Did Henry VIII love Anne Boleyn?" is a question that is impossible to answer. Only Henry VIII would be able to answer it. However, it's a question that often comes up, and it's one I want to explore.

Anne Boleyn was recalled from serving Queen Claude, the wife of King Francis I of France, in late 1521. Not long after her debut at the English court, Anne became romantically involved with Henry Percy, son and heir of the 5ᵗʰ Earl of Northumberland, as I explained in the previous chapter. According to George Cavendish, Cardinal Wolsey's servant, the king found out about the romance and was "much offended" because of his own "secret affection". The King ordered Wolsey to put a stop to it. Wolsey and Percy's father berated Percy, and a marriage match with Mary Talbot, a daughter of the Earl of Shrewsbury, was arranged for him instead.

Now, we don't know for sure that the king put a stop to the romance because he was himself interested in Anne. Cavendish was writing with the hindsight of knowing that the king did eventually fall in love with Anne and marry her. What is more likely is that the negotiations for Anne to marry James Butler were still ongoing (and the king was involved in them) and that Percy was due to marry Mary Talbot. The couple's "folly" threatened these marriage plans.

It is impossible to date the start of Henry VIII's interest in Anne Boleyn. David Starkey believes that Anne first caught the king's eye in the winter of 1524/5 as that fits in with Cavendish's account of Wolsey's fall. Eric Ives, however, dates the start of their courtship to Shrovetide 1526, when the king rode out to the Shrovetide joust with the motto *"Declare je nos"* (Declare I dare not) embroidered on his costume along with an image of a heart engulfed in flames. It may, however, simply have been a chivalric theme which had nothing to do with the king's love life. Whatever the truth of the matter, in August 1527 Henry VIII applied to the pope for a dispensation to cover the impediment of affinity in the first degree – Henry wanted to marry a woman who was closely related (mother or sister) of a woman he'd already been involved with sexually.

So sometime before August 1527, Henry VIII had proposed to Anne Boleyn, and she had sent him a "costly Diamond, and the Ship in which the solitary Damsel is tossed about" which Henry described in a love letter he wrote to Anne as her "humble submission", her 'yes'.

But what do we know of their courtship?

Unfortunately, very little. There is not one iota of evidence for the idea that Anne's father and uncle acted as pimps and pushed the sisters, Mary and Anne Boleyn, at the king. There is also no evidence for the idea that Anne set out to seduce and manipulate the king. What we do know, from the king's love letters to Anne, which are unfortunately undated, is that the king pursued Anne, bombarding her with letters and gifts, that she retreated from court to her family home of Hever Castle, that he offered her the opportunity to be his official mistress, that she refused and that he eventually proposed marriage to her and she submitted.

Was this love or lust?

Again, it's impossible to say, but in June 1528, during an outbreak of sweating sickness, a disease that could kill in hours, Anne became ill. The king heard the news that his sweetheart was ill and wrote her a panicked letter. My dear friend, author Sandra Vasoli, has held and looked at Henry VIII's love letters to Anne Boleyn in the Vatican Archives and she noticed a marked contrast between this letter and the others that the king sent to Anne. Sandra described it as "visually a mess" because the ink is smeared, there are sprays of ink where the nib of the quill caught on the parchment, and there are ink blots. It was a hurried letter written by a panicked man. Its appearance is evidence of Henry VIII's terror on hearing the news of Anne's illness. This surely points to him loving Anne.

He also waited over six years for her, went through all the stress of the Great Matter, making enemies of the Pope and Holy Roman Empire, risked excommunication and finally broke with Rome to be with her. A bit much for lust. He could have taken a mistress of two to satisfy his lust.

You could argue that this was all because Henry was intent on having a son and Catherine of Aragon couldn't give him one, but then Henry, I'm sure, could have legitimised Henry Fitzroy with the Pope's blessing. But he wanted Anne.

Let's go back to his pursuit of her.

Thomas Wyatt, a man who appears to have been in love with Anne himself at one point, appears to describe the king's pursuit of his wife's maid of honour in his poem "Whoso List to Hunt". In the poem, the poet is hunting a deer but has to withdraw from the hunt when another hunter claims the hind. He writes of how the words "Caesar's I am" are written about her neck. Wyatt is describing how he had to give up on Anne when the king, Caesar, claimed her for himself. Henry VIII being the hunter, and Anne a powerless hind hunted down by him and then possessed by him, when combined with the king's letters, his gifts and Anne's retreat from court, have led to the idea that Anne can claim to be a member of the #metoo campaign, that she was a victim of sexual harassment. Karen Lindsey, in her book *Divorced, Beheaded, Survived: A Feminist Reinterpretation Of The Wives Of Henry VIII*, writes "Today, Henry's approach to Anne would be instantly identifiable as sexual harassment. Anne however, had no social or legal recourse against the man who ruled the country. She continued, as so many women before and since have done, to dodge her pursuer's advances while sparing his feelings. It didn't work."

I think the keyword here is "today". Today, a business owner bombarding an employee with love letters and gifts after she has declined his advances and taken time off work would be accused of sexual harassment, and rightly so. But Henry VIII and Anne Boleyn were 16th century people. The king was expected to get what he wanted, and Anne was unusual in saying "no" to him. Once the king proposed to her, she said yes, and from that point, she seems to have put her all into supporting his quest for an annulment and fighting to be his wife and queen.

Did she love him?

Probably not from the start, but I think she did come to do so. It's easy for us to forget that Henry VIII was quite a catch. At this point, he was handsome, he was charming, he was witty, he was intelligent, he was athletic, he was a gifted Renaissance Prince. Anne was intelligent and well-educated, and they shared interests – architecture, music, theology... What wasn't there to love about the king, except that he had a wife?

I've heard it said that Henry could not have loved Anne because he ended up hating her and executing her. That real love can't lead to a man standing by while his wife is framed for crimes she didn't commit and then beheaded as a result. But we all know couples that started off deeply in love and somehow ended up hating each other. We've all read about cases where a man has murdered his wife, and sometimes his children, and yet friends and neighbours all testify about how happy they used to be. People can go from having stars in their eyes, hearts floating around their head, being head over heels in love and being prepared to give their life for their loved one to wanting the object of their affections to die a slow, painful death. We hear about "crimes of passion". Love really does turn to hate. Does that mean it never properly existed? No, of course not, it's just that feelings change. People are human; they can make mistakes and hurt the people they love, they can change and not be the same person, there can be outside pressures that come to bear on the relationship. When we realise that the love of our life is not who we thought they were, when the person we have invested time, effort and feelings into lets us down or changes then we can get angry, and anger can turn to hate.

When I first got married, a friend quoted the Bible verse "Do not let the sun go down while you are still angry..." (Ephesians 4: 26) to me and I have tried to keep to it. It's wise advice because if you go to bed angry, then that anger festers and turns into resentment, which, in time, could turn to hate. Your mind brings forth other episodes from the past, and you get angrier and angrier. This may well have happened in Henry and Anne's marriage.

Henry also seems to have been the kind of person that could flip from love to hate if he felt let down in any way. Look at Thomas More who went from loved and respected father figure to a victim of the axeman when he refused to do what the king wanted, and Catherine of Aragon and Mary who were Henry's loved and pampered wife and daughter but who defied him and so were treated abominably. People who let him down or defied him in some way went from being loved to being hated just like that.

We can't know what happened in Henry and Anne's marriage. We know that it was a relationship based on love and that this led to Anne being worried and jealous when her husband showed an interest in other women. We know that Henry was obsessed with having a surviving male heir. Did Anne's jealousy annoy the king? Did her failure to provide him with a son make him feel let down by her? Or did he begin to believe that the marriage was wrong and against God's laws? Did their relationship become more storms than sunshine? Did it all become too much of a stress and effort for the king? Did he come to believe that he'd made a huge mistake turning the country upside down and making enemies so that he could marry Anne?

It's impossible to say, but it's easy to understand how all of those stresses could undermine his love for his second wife. Hate is a strong feeling, just as love is, and I think we can only truly hate someone if we have loved them at some point. They are two extremes. Just my view, of course!

Historians are not in agreement about who was ultimately responsible for Anne Boleyn's fall, whether Henry VIII ordered Cromwell to remove Anne at any cost or whether Cromwell manipulated the king and made him believe that Anne had been unfaithful. I'm in the 'Henry's to blame" camp, but either way, I believe that the lover who penned that distraught love letter came to hate his wife and let her be executed on 19th May 1536.

Notes and Sources

Cavendish, George (1827) The Life of Cardinal Wolsey, Second Edition, Harding & Lepard, p. 121.

Starkey, David (2004) *Six Wives: The Queens of Henry VIII*, Vintage.

Ives, Eric (2005) *The Life and Death of Anne Boleyn*, Wiley-Blackwell.

"Sandra Vasoli on the love letters of Henry VIII", talk on 6 January 2015, The Tudor Society.

Lindsey, Karen (1996) *Divorced, Beheaded, Survived: A Feminist Reinterpretation Of The Wives Of Henry VIII*, Da Capo Press.

When did Anne Boleyn say yes to Henry VIII?

I wrote this article after attending historian David Starkey's talk "Henry VIII: The First Brexiteer" at the Festival Theatre, Hever Castle, in 2018. It was a wonderful talk, both entertaining and educational, and in it, Dr Starkey shared his view on the dating of Anne Boleyn's acceptance of Henry VIII's proposal of marriage. It is something that he has mentioned before in his book on the six wives, but I hadn't discussed it on the Anne Boleyn Files before so I thought I'd share it with my followers.

As Dr Starkey explained, Henry VIII's love letters to Anne Boleyn, which are held now in the Vatican Archives, are not dated. There are several theories regarding the order in which they were written and when they were written, but only David Starkey, I believe, goes as far as to give a firm date for Anne's acceptance of the king's proposal, which she signified by sending him a jewelled trinket. Henry VIII described it in his letter as "the costly Diamond, and the Ship in which the solitary Damsel is tossed about". Henry thanked Anne for the gift, "but chiefly for the fine interpretation, and too humble submission", i.e. for her submission to his will. Eric Ives explains that "For centuries the ship had been a symbol of protection – the ark which rescued

Noah from the destroying deluge; the diamond – as the Roman de la Rose had said – spoke of a 'heart as hard as diamond, steadfast and nothing pliant'."

Now, this letter was written in French, and this is where things get interesting. As Ives and Starkey both point out, Henry VIII thanks Anne for "l'etrene [étrenne]", rather than "le cadeau". If you don't know French, "cadeau" means gift or present and so does "étrenne". However, "étrennes" are more specific than "cadeaux", they are usually gifts given at New Year. Starkey believes, therefore, that Anne said "yes" to Henry VIII on 1st January 1527, 1527 fitting with the king's claim that he had been in love with her for a year. Eric Ives talks about the use of "étrenne" in the letter, stating that "the word was acquiring an implication of 'novelty' or 'special occasion'", but that it "was also developing a second meaning – 'virginity'." Ives believes that by using this word, rather than "cadeau", "Henry could be picking up on Anne's assertion that her maidenhead was reserved for her future husband" and that by giving Henry this gift, and thereby accepting his proposal, she was offering her maidenhead to him. Interesting!

So, Starkey dates the acceptance to 1st January 1527 and the start of Henry's interest in Anne to 1525, but what does Eric Ives think? Well, he believes that Henry began his "courtly pursuit" of Anne at Shrovetide 1526 and that the couple agreed to marry in summer 1527. Does it matter? Well, as Ives points out, if you go with the earlier date then you make Anne "the catalyst for the rejection of Katherine", whereas if you go with the later dating then it's two years after Henry had ceased to have sexual relations with his first wife, and Anne is more of a solution to the king's matrimonial woes rather than a cause.

While we cannot definitively date Anne Boleyn's acceptance of Henry VIII's marriage proposal, we do know that she had said 'yes' before August 1527 because that is when Henry asked the Pope for a dispensation. The dispensation was for the king to marry "one with whom he had already contracted affinity in the first degree through illicit intercourse", i.e. to cover the impediment created by marrying a woman with whose sister or mother he had already had sexual intercourse. When Sir George Throckmorton told the king that it was rumoured that "ye have meddled both with the mother and the sister" of Anne Boleyn, Henry VIII stated "Never with the mother", so the relationship the dispensation referred to was the one with Mary Boleyn.

Notes and Sources

"Henry VIII: The First Brexiteer", a talk by Dr David Starkey at the Festival Theatre, Hever Castle, 8 August 2018.

ed. Oldys, William (1745) *The Harleian miscellany: or, A collection of scarce, curious, and entertaining pamphlets and tracts, as well in manuscript as in print*, Volume III, p. 54, Lettre V.

Ives, Eric (2004) *The Life and Death of Anne Boleyn*, Wiley-Blackwell Publishing, pp. 88-90.

Kelly, Henry Ansgar (2004) *The Matrimonial Trials of Henry VIII*, Wipf & Stock Publishers, pp. 42-3.

Catherine of Aragon –
right to fight?

In 2016, on the anniversary of Catherine of Aragon's burial at Peterborough Abbey in 1536, I posed the question "Was Catherine of Aragon right in fighting for her marriage and not accepting the annulment?" with this article on the Anne Boleyn Files.

Catherine of Aragon experienced her last pregnancy in 1518, and it ended in the birth of a stillborn daughter. Out of at least six pregnancies, Catherine had experienced four stillbirths, the birth of a son who had died at 52 days old, and the birth of a surviving daughter, Mary. This catalogue of obstetric disasters had led her husband to believe that their marriage was wrong in the eyes of God and that he should never have married his brother's widow, thereby breaking the law laid out in Leviticus:

> "And if a man shall take his brother's wife, it [is] an unclean thing: he hath uncovered his brother's nakedness; they shall be childless."

A Hebrew scholar, Robert Wakefield, had told Henry VIII that the original Hebrew of that law in Leviticus was that the marriage would be without "sons", rather than being "childless", so Henry was convinced that he and Catherine had sinned and that the pope's dispensation for their marriage should never have been issued. Catherine did not agree. She argued that her marriage to Arthur had never been consummated and so there was no impediment to their marriage or anything wrong with it. Henry was not convinced, he felt that the tragedies of their lost children were proof.

It wasn't as if annulments were out of the ordinary. In his TV series, "Sex and the Church", historian Diarmaid MacCulloch looked at the Church's involvement in marriage and talked about the case of Robert de Mowbray, Earl of Northumberland, and his wife Maude in the 11th century. At the time, Church law was that no-one could marry within seven degrees of consanguinity. This made it difficult for the Normans in England because it meant that everyone they knew was out-of-bounds. Robert and Maude were Normans and were distant cousins affected by this law, so they got a dispensation for their marriage. The marriage turned sour within two years due to Robert rebelling against the king and being branded a traitor. Maude wanted out of the marriage and so appealed to the pope for an annulment, alleging that as they were cousins that their marriage was against Church law and so should be annulled. She was granted an annulment and then went on to apply for a further dispensation to marry another of her cousins, Nigel d'Aubigny. Maude was unable to provide Nigel with an heir so he promptly argued for an annulment so that he could remarry. More recently, Louis XII of France had had his marriage to his first wife, Joan, annulled by the pope so that he could marry Charles VIII's widow, Anne of Brittany. So, Henry VIII's request for an annulment wasn't unusual, and the pope would have granted it if Catherine hadn't opposed it.

The pope was caught between a rock and a hard place. He wanted to keep Henry VIII on side but also wanted to avoid upsetting Emperor Charles V, Catherine's nephew, so when papal legate, Cardinal Lorenzo Campeggio, arrived in England in 1528 ready to hear the case for the annulment, he met with Catherine and advised her to join a convent, something which would allow the marriage to be annulled easily. However, Catherine believed that she was Henry's true wife and queen, and would not agree to taking the veil.

If only Catherine had accepted the annulment and gone to a convent, how history would have been different. Her daughter, Mary, probably would not have been made illegitimate (the marriage having been made in good faith) and would not have gone through the stress of having to defy her father, which included being threatened by members of her father's council. Eustace Chapuys, the imperial ambassador, was so worried at one point about Mary's safety that he advised her to submit to her father, reassuring her that "God looked more into the intentions than into the deeds of men." The stress that Mary experienced seems to have had a major impact on her health and must have also had an impact on her as a person, her personality, and the woman she would become later.

Of course, Henry's quest for an annulment, due to Catherine's opposition, led to him breaking with Rome and becoming the supreme head of the Church of England. This, in turn, led to the executions of those who would not sign the oath of supremacy (including the Carthusian monks, Bishop Fisher and Thomas More), reformers (those who Catherine viewed as heretics) influencing the king, and the dissolution of the monasteries. Catherine's defiance of her husband had far-reaching consequences, something she could never have predicted. But Catherine was in an impossible situation. If she obeyed her husband, then she would be compromising her faith. She had made vows to her husband before God, and she was bound to her husband for life. As Garrett Mattingly puts it, "she was Henry's wife; it would have been a sin to deny it", but, "would it not also have been a sin to rebel against her husband?" Her conscience would not let her abandon her marriage because it put her soul, and that of her husband, into mortal peril.

Catherine's decision, and what it led to, the consequences

it had for her husband, her daughter and England as a whole, haunted Catherine in her final days. Eustace Chapuys, a man who had become a good friend to Catherine and Mary, visited Catherine in her final illness, reporting back to the Emperor:

> "Out of the four days I staid [stayed] at Kimbolton not one passed without my paying her an equally long visit, the whole of her commendations and charges being reduced to this: her personal concerns and will; the state of Your Majesty's affairs abroad; complaints of her own misfortunes and those of the Princess, her daughter, as well as of the delay in the proposed remedy, which delay, she said, was the cause of infinite evil among all honest and worthy people of this country, of great damage to their persons and property, and of great danger to their souls."

Chapuys assured her that what had happened in England "could in nowise be imputed to her" and was relieved that "This speech of mine made the Queen happy and contented, whereas formerly she had certain conscientious fears as to whether the evils and heresies of this country might not have been principally caused by the divorce affair."

In her final days, Catherine wrote a letter to Henry VIII. It no longer exists, and it is not known for sure whether the transcripts which appear in later sources, like Nicholas Sander's *De Origine ac Progressu schismatis Anglicani* and Nicholas Harpsfield's *A Treatise on the Pretended Divorce Between Henry VIII and Catharine of Aragon* is authentic. The words ring true, though, when we consider Chapuys' reports of their conversations in those last days:

> "My most dear lord, king and husband,
> The hour of my death now drawing on, the tender love I owe you forceth me, my case being such, to commend myself to you, and to put you in remembrance with a few words of the health and safeguard of your soul which you ought to

prefer before all worldly matters, and before the care and pampering of your body, for the which you have cast me into many calamities and yourself into many troubles. For my part I pardon you everything and I wish to devoutly pray to God that He will pardon you also. For the rest, I commend unto you our daughter Mary, beseeching you to be a good father unto her, as I have heretofore desired. I entreat you also, on behalf of my maids, to give them marriage portions, which is not much, they being but three. For all my other servants, I solicit the wages due to them, and a year or more, lest they be unprovided for. Lastly, I make this vow, that mine eyes desire you above all things."

It is a moving letter. Even if it is fictional, we know that Catherine never stopped loving Henry VIII and she always saw herself as his true wife and queen. To her dying day, she wanted to save Henry from himself.

Now, this article doesn't go into all the points, but I hope that it's provoked you to think about Catherine. Could she have done anything differently? Should she have acted differently? Was she in an impossible situation? Could she have reconciled her faith and the annulment? Should she have put her country and her daughter before her feelings or would that have been putting her soul at peril? Was she disobedient and defiant? Should she have submitted to her husband and king?

Notes and Sources

"Sex and the Church", TV series written and presented by Diarmaid MacCulloch, BBC Two, 2015.

Loades, David (2009) *The Six Wives of Henry VIII*, Amberley, p. 45, quoting BL Cotton MS Otho C X, f. 185. The Divorce Tracts of Henry VIII, eds. J. Surtz and V Murphy, xiii.

'Spain: January 1536, 1-20', in Calendar of State Papers, Spain, Volume 5 Part 2, 1536-1538, ed. Pascual de Gayangos (London, 1888), pp. 1-10. British History Online http://

www.british-history.ac.uk/cal-state-papers/spain/vol5/no2/pp1-10

Ibid., pp. 170-187. British History Online http://www.british-history.ac.uk/cal-state-papers/spain/vol5/no2/pp170-187

Mattingly, Garrett (1942) *Catherine of Aragon*, Jonathan Cape, pp. 306, 308.

Sander, Nicholas (1877) *Rise and Growth of the Anglican Schism* [*De Origine ac Progressu schismatis Anglicani*], Burns and Oates, p. 131, originally published in 1586.

Harpsfield, Nicholas (1878) *A Treatise on the Pretended Divorce Between Henry VIII. and Catharine of Aragon*, Camden Society, p. 199-200, written in the 16th century.

Anne Boleyn's dog Purkoy

I was inspired to write this article after having to have our nineteen-year-old cat put down due to kidney failure. It's a heartbreaking decision to have to make. You want and need to end the animal's suffering, but you don't want to lose your beloved pet. The grief I felt made me think about Anne Boleyn and how she must have felt when she lost her little dog in 1534.

Anne Boleyn had a lapdog called Purkoy, a name that came from the French 'pourquoi', meaning 'why?'. The little dog was originally given to Sir Francis Bryan, Anne's cousin, by Lady Lisle as a New Year's gift. She'd given the dog to Bryan on the advice of John Husee because the Lisles needed Bryan's help. Lady Lisle had been fond of Purkoy, but she had to follow Husee's advice:

"But madam, there is no remedy, your ladyship must needs depart with your little Purkoy, the which I knew well shall grive [grieve] your ladyship not a little."

However, Bryan ended up passing the gift on to the queen. He wrote to Lord Lisle on 20th January 1534 asking him to thank his wife for the gift but explaining what had happened:

"…it may please your Lordship to give her hearty thanks on my behalf for her little dog, which was so proper and so well liked by the Queen that it remained not above an hour in my hands but that her Grace took it from me."

Unfortunately, Anne's beloved Purkoy was killed in an accident just a few months later. Thomas Broke wrote to Lady Lisle on 18ᵗʰ December 1534, advising her on gifts for the Queen and passing on the advice of Margery Horsman, one of the Queen's ladies:

> "Also she saith that the Queen's Grace setteth much store by a pretty dog, and her Grace delighted so much in little Purkoy that after he was dead of a fall there durst nobody tell her Grace of it, till it pleased the King's Highness to tell her Grace of it."

Broke went on to advise that Anne preferred a male dog to a female. It is not known what kind of dog Purkoy was, but perhaps a toy spaniel or toy poodle. Anne obviously loved her little dog, and it must have been hard for her to cope with the idea of her beloved pet being killed in such a tragic accident. She must have been devastated.

Anne Boleyn also had a greyhound. Although it is often said that her greyhound was called Urian and was given to her by Urian Brereton, brother of William Brereton, I have found no evidence of this. In Henry VIII's Privy Purse Expenses, there is a record of a farmer being paid 10 shillings for a cow which had been killed by two greyhounds, one belonging to Urian Brereton and the other belonging to Anne:

> "Itm the same daye paied for A Cowe that Uryren a Breretons greyhounde and my ladye Annes killed – x s." 25 September 1530

Although this could be read as one of the greyhounds being called "Urian", but belonging to the Breretons, there were two dogs involved, and I'm not sure that Urian Brereton or William Brereton would have called their dog "Urian". It is more likely that "Uryren a Breretons greyhounde" means "Urian Brereton's greyhound" or "Urian, a Brereton greyhound". I am convinced that the cow was killed by two greyhounds, both unnamed: one belonging to Urian Brereton and the other belonging to Anne Boleyn.

Notes and Sources

ed. St. Clare Byrne, Muriel (1981) *The Lisle Letters*, Volume 2, University of Chicago Press, pp.21-22, letter 109; p.30, letter 114; p.331, letter 299a.

ed. Nicolas, Nicholas Harris (1827) *The privy purse expenses of King Henry the Eighth, from November 1529, to December 1532*, William Pickering, p.74.

The spitefully ambitious
Anne Boleyn

In January 2014, Susan Bordo, author of *The Creation of Anne Boleyn*, drew attention on her Facebook page to a review of the RSC stage adaptations of Hilary Mantel's *Wolf Hall* and *Bring Up the Bodies*. The review by Morning Star included the comment "Lydia Leonard's spitefully ambitious Anne Boleyn – a wife who one feels any king would be justified in beheading" - Oh dear. But, it did make me think…

Now, Mantel was writing from Thomas Cromwell's perspective, and the Boleyns did not get much sympathy, so we have to take that into account. Another review, this time by the *Daily Mail*, talked of the Boleyn family being "burdened by a feckless brother", when, in reality, George Boleyn, was anything but feckless. But, I digress. While I would disagree with anyone who says that Anne Boleyn's execution was justified, that it was karma, and she deserved it – and I would hate to see a portrayal of Anne which made the reader/viewer/audience feel that Henry was justified in doing what he did to her – there is no denying that Anne was ambitious and that she could be spiteful at times.

As much as I admire Anne Boleyn, she had her flaws. She's a huge part of my life, nobody coming to my house or reading my blog or Facebook page could miss the fact that I am completely fascinated with this woman. The late Eric Ives described Anne as the third woman in his life after his wife and daughter, and I know just what he means. Anne has got under my skin, as have her whole family, I spend every day researching the Boleyns, and I love it, they are my passion. But, and it's a big 'but', I do not put them on pedestals. I would say that it's their flaws as much as their admirable qualities which make me so fascinated with them. Here was a queen consort who was so human. Yes, she had admirable qualities – she was ambitious and highly intelligent, she put her neck on the line to help people (for example the reformer Nicholas Bourbon), she helped to promote religious reform and the dissemination of the Bible in English, she was charitable and was concerned with poor relief and education, she was a patron of the Arts…. – but she also had a fiery temper, she let her mouth run away with her and said exactly what she thought, and it is reported that she said spiteful things about Catherine and Mary. We cannot ignore that side of her character.

An example of Anne's spiteful side is when, in 1534, according to Eustace Chapuys, the imperial ambassador, Anne claimed that if Henry ever left her as regent while he was away, then she would have Princess Mary killed. George, Anne's brother, stepped in and warned her that an action like that would offend the king, but Anne said that "she cared not if she did, even if she were to be burnt or flayed alive in consequence." Another example is in 1531, when, before she was queen, Anne "said to one of the Queen's ladies that she wished all the Spaniards in the world were in the sea; and on the other replying, that, for the honor of the Queen, she should not say so, she said that she did not care anything for the Queen, and would rather see her hanged than acknowledge her as her mistress." Harsh things to say about her former mistress and Henry VIII's daughter. Her words were spiteful, unwise and not becoming of a queen, or queen-in-waiting, but it doesn't mean that Anne was bad through and through. She was frustrated, she was angry that these women were not doing what they were told, that they wouldn't just go away, and while that is no excuse for Anne's words, it does make them understandable. Eric Ives writes of how "Anne was ranting, not thinking" and that "Anne's language was violent and threatening, but this sprang not from malevolence but from self-defence", and he has a point. Anne had tried her hardest to build bridges with Mary and Mary had rejected her, and rather rudely too. Yes, Anne should have kept her temper, she should have kept her thoughts to herself, but she didn't. We're all spiteful at one time or another, but Anne was queen, and it was up to her to set a good example. Of course, we have to take into account Chapuys' bias here and the fact that he may have exaggerated her words somewhat. Did she even say them? We don't know.

Anne Boleyn is often blamed for the ill-treatment of Catherine and Mary, and the executions of the Carthusian monks and men like Thomas More and Bishop Fisher, but I feel that this is going too far. After Henry offered her marriage and the crown, Anne set her heart on being queen. She'd been raised to be 'somebody', and she appears to have had natural ambition and drive. I believe that Henry convinced her that his marriage to Catherine of Aragon was not valid and that the Pope should never have issued a dispensation for it because it was against God's laws. Henry appears to have convinced himself of that, and it would have been easy for God's anointed sovereign to have convinced Anne of that, he was her king after all.

Anne and Henry did everything in their power to make things go their way, to do what they thought was God's plan, but Anne cannot be blamed for the executions of those men, that was up to Henry. Perhaps some people see her whispering evil plans in Henry's ear, manipulating him to do dastardly deeds, but Henry VIII was not a man to let himself be manipulated by anyone, never mind a woman. People like the Carthusian monks, More and Fisher had to be punished because they were disobeying their king: they were rebelling and betraying him, and Henry saw that as treason. It was the same with Catherine and Mary;

they had to be punished for defying him. Anne encouraged the ill-treatment of Mary, and it was something she later regretted. On the evening before her execution, Anne fell on her knees before Lady Kingston and "requested her to go in her name to the Lady Mary, to kneel before her in like manner, and beg of her to pardon an unfortunate woman the many wrongs she had done her." And Mary's treatment got worse after Anne's death. It was all down to Henry VIII. Henry was willing to acknowledge Mary as his daughter and to mend their relationship if she toed the line, it was that simple in his eyes.

Anne can be blamed for supporting Henry, for letting these things happen, but what could she have done? Henry did not like meddling from the women in his life. As Ives points out, blaming Anne for Mary's ill-treatment "made it much easier for Charles V [Catherine of Aragon's nephew] to keep up some civil relationship with Henry" so Chapuys could paint Anne as the bad guy. It was also easier for Mary to blame her step-mother for the way she was being treated, rather than her father and king.

There is a moving scene in the play *Fallen in Love: The Secret Heart of Anne Boleyn*. In it, George Boleyn is consumed with guilt and grief over the brutal executions of the Carthusian monks and the things that have happened as a consequence of the rise of the Boleyns, and he tries to talk to Anne about it. Anne too is upset, but she sees the brutalities as the unavoidable cost of her rise to queen. We cannot know how the real Anne felt, whether she felt guilt and remorse over what happened as a result of Henry's quest to marry her or whether she saw the deaths as unavoidable and for the greater good. We cannot get inside her head, we have no sources to tell us how she felt, and so we cannot judge her. If we are to blame someone for those atrocities, then we have to blame the person who was responsible for them: Henry VIII, and even then we have to understand that he saw those people as traitors who deserved to die. We live in a very different world, and it is impossible for us to understand Henry VIII.

The Anne I have come to know through my research was

definitely ambitious and was spiteful at times, but she wasn't "spitefully ambitious", that makes her sound like someone who was spiteful through and through and who used spite to realise her ambitions. I don't see that at all. She didn't set out to be queen at all costs, she didn't manipulate Henry VIII into making her queen, but she did everything she could to be queen once that was on offer – there's a difference.

Anne did not deserve to die in 1536, her death was not justified, and I find it sad that any portrayal of her would make people think that. However, she also was not an angel, and we can't whitewash her. Let's accept that she was human, that she was downright nasty sometimes, but she was also loved and respected, and she certainly did not deserve to be framed, to have her name blackened and to die such a horrible death.

Notes and Sources

The Creation of Anne Boleyn Facebook page - https://www.facebook.com/thecreationofanneboleyn/

"Theatre: Wolf Hall/Bring Up the Bodies", Morning Star, 14 January 2014.

"Superb! A groaning banquet of political shenanigans: Quentin Letts reviews the stage adaptation of Hilary Mantel's award-winning novel", the Daily Mail, 8 January 2014.

Ives, Eric (2004) *The Life and Death of Anne Boleyn*, Wiley-Blackwell, pp. xiv, 197, 198.

'Spain: January 1531, 1-10', in Calendar of State Papers, Spain, Volume 4 Part 2, 1531-1533, ed. Pascual de Gayangos (London, 1882), pp. 1-17. British History Online http://www.british-history.ac.uk/cal-state-papers/spain/vol4/no2/pp1-17.

'Spain: June 1534, 16-30', in Calendar of State Papers, Spain, Volume 5 Part 1, 1534-1535, ed. Pascual de Gayangos (London, 1886), pp. 192-200. British History Online http://www.british-history.ac.uk/cal-state-papers/spain/vol5/no1/pp192-200.

Lingard, John (1820) *The History of England, from the First Invasion By the Romans to the Accession of Mary*, Volume IV, p.244; Cassell, Peter (1873) *Cassell's Illustrated History of England*: Volume 2, p.6.; Speed, John (1611) *The History of Great Britain.*

"Henry VIII's Council Bullies Mary" by Claire Ridgway, Anne Boleyn Files, 15 June, 2012, https://www.theanneboleynfiles. com/15-june-1536-henry-viiis-council-bullies-mary/.

In April 1536, Henry wrote "As to the legitimation of our daughter Mary, we answered that if she will submit to our grace without wrestling against the determination of our laws, we will acknowledge her and use her as our daughter; but we would not be directed or pressed herein, nor have any other order devised for her entertainment than should proceed from the inclination of our own heart." 'Henry VIII: April 1536, 21-25', in Letters and Papers, Foreign and Domestic, Henry VIII, Volume 10, January-June 1536, ed. James Gairdner (London, 1887), pp. 287-310. British History Online http://www.british-history.ac.uk/letters-papers-hen8/vol10/pp287-310.

"Fallen in Love: The Secret Heart of Anne Boleyn", Joanna Carrick, Red Rose Chain Theatre Company, performed at the Tower of London, May 2013.

Anne Boleyn – No innocent victim, apparently

With running an Anne Boleyn blog, making videos about her and having written books on her, I come across the following views on a fairly regular basis:

- Anne was no innocent victim
- She knew exactly what she was doing
- She played a game and lost
- She knew the dangers/risks
- She didn't deserve to die, but she was far from an innocent victim
- She was a whore who took a man from his marriage and got her just desserts
- She got what she deserved
- She may have been innocent of the crimes, but her death was karma

The general idea I get from these types of commenters is that even if Anne was innocent of the charges against her in 1536, she can't be viewed as an innocent victim because her fall was her own fault; she was overly ambitious and set her sights on a married man because she wanted the crown. Pride comes before a fall, don't you know?

I'm sorry, but I struggle with this type of view. These comments make me very cross.

Anne Boleyn is not a fictional character. She's not a *Game of Thrones* character. Anne was a living, breathing person whose life ended on a scaffold when her head was removed from her body by a sword. Yes, her head was cut off. Before that brutal end – and it wasn't a fake CGI death, it was real – she had had to come to terms with the fact that she had been sentenced to death for crimes she did not commit, that five innocent men had lost their lives because of a plot against her, that her daughter would grow up without her mother and believing her mother to have been a traitor, that her family name would be blackened by the charges against her, that her parents were losing a son and a daughter, that her husband had already replaced her... Can you imagine what she went through in those last days? I can't even begin to imagine.

But, we can't feel sorry for her because she knew exactly what she was doing – right?

Yes, apparently, back in the 1520s, this young, power-hungry woman with her eye on the crown set her sights on Henry VIII – a married man no less – seduced him and manipulated him, all the time knowing that she risked this bad end. The crown was worth it all. She knew the risks! Yes, she knew she risked death because this had happened before, hadn't it?

Erm, no, since when had a queen consort been executed?

How could Anne have been aware of the risks? How could she have known what she was doing, what she was letting herself in for? Even if we go for the sexual predator-type Anne Boleyn doing all she could to get the crown, how could she ever know that her actions would lead to her being on the scaffold on 19th May 1536? I just can't see how it can be said that "she knew what she was doing". There was no precedent; she wasn't one of Henry VIII's later queens who'd seen how the earlier ones had been treated.

But this sexual predator-type Anne Boleyn doesn't even fit

with the evidence we have regarding her early relationship with Henry VIII. OK, so we've only got Henry VIII's love letters to Anne and not her replies, but these surviving letters do give us some insight into their courtship, and it is possible to 'read between the lines' at points. It is clear that Henry set his sights on Anne and that he then wooed her, going all out to obtain her, wanting her to become his mistress, then his official mistress, and then, after her refusal of this offer, wanting her to become his wife. He was obsessed with her, he wanted Anne at all costs, and it is clear that Anne rebuffed him at first, that she even left the court and retreated to the family home at Hever in Kent. But Henry didn't take no for an answer; he was king after all. One author goes as far as to depict Anne Boleyn as a victim of sexual harassment, basing this idea on Thomas Wyatt the Elder's famous poem "Whoso List to Hunt":

> *Whoso list to hunt, I know where is an hind,*
> *But as for me, hélas, I may no more.*
> *The vain travail hath wearied me so sore,*
> *I am of them that farthest cometh behind.*
> *Yet may I by no means my wearied mind*
> *Draw from the deer, but as she fleeth afore*
> *Fainting I follow. I leave off therefore,*
> *Since in a net I seek to hold the wind.*
> *Who list her hunt, I put him out of doubt,*
> *As well as I may spend his time in vain.*
> *And graven with diamonds in letters plain*
> *There is written, her fair neck round about:*
> *Noli me tangere, for Caesar's I am,*
> *And wild for to hold, though I seem tame.*

In this poem, which is based on Petrarch's "Una Candida Cerva", Wyatt starts with a challenge, telling those who want to hunt that he knows the location of a hind, but he goes on to say that he is weary of the chase and that his hunt failed, that the hind was claimed by Caesar: "*Noli me tangere* [don't touch me]," says the hind, "for I am Caesar's. This "wild to hold" hind can't be Wyatt's, she doesn't belong to him. It is thought that this poem is about Wyatt's feelings for Anne Boleyn, and, in an article in The Guardian, Carol Rumens writes:

> "But this is still a love-poem, and nowhere more obviously than in that final, para-rhymed couplet, where, having quoted the injunction, Noli me tangere, the hind describes herself as "wild for to hold". This instantly transports us to a hinterland of erotic excitement, and registers the extent of the poet's loss and hurt, now that the King has claimed Wyatt's dear as his own."

It's a poem about lost love, but is Wyatt saying something even more by depicting Anne Boleyn as a hind? Is he seeing her as a quarry hunted down by the King, ensnared by him and becoming his whether she liked it or not? Being owned by him, even labelled by him as his possession. Perhaps that's reading too much into it, but Karen Lindsey, author of *Divorced, Beheaded, Survived: A Feminist Reinterpretation Of The Wives Of Henry VIII* certainly sees Anne as Henry's victim:

> "Today, Henry's approach to Anne would be instantly identifiable as sexual harassment. Anne however, had no social or legal recourse against the man who ruled the country. She continued, as so many women before and since have done, to dodge her pursuer's advances while sparing his feelings. It didn't work... It was a hellish position. Could she really tell the king to his face that she had no interest in him? She could reiterate her desire to keep her chastity and her honor, but clearly he didn't respect that. She could ignore his letters and stay away from court, but he refused to take the hint. To offer him the outright insult he asked for would be to risk not only her own but her father's and brother's careers at court. She undoubtedly kept hoping he would tire of the chase and transfer his attentions to some newer lady-in-waiting.

But he didn't and she was trapped: there was no chance of her making a good marriage when every eligible nobleman knew the king wanted her. She began to realize she would have to give in. [as Wyatt wrote in his poem 'Whoso list to hunt'] 'Nole me tangere, for Caesar's I am'.

Virtually every account of Anne's story cites the poem, yet its central image is ignored. Anne was a creature being hunted, and hunted by the king — like the buck he had killed and so proudly sent to her. There could be no refuge from the royal assault; no one would risk protecting her from Henry's chase. She could run, hide, dodge for a time, but the royal hunter would eventually track down his prey. And he would destroy her. The hunt was not an archaic metaphor in sixteenth century life, it was a vivid integral part of that life and everyone knew what happened to the wild creature at the end."

You may feel that Lindsey is going too far, and you may believe that Henry's wooing caused Anne to fall in love with him, but then it still appears that he was the instigator. He chased her; she rebuffed him; he made her a good offer while also wooing the hell out of her, and she accepted it. Only then did she start to fight for her position, support the King in his quest for an annulment and support his treatment of his first wife and daughter. I haven't seen one iota of evidence that Anne set out to seduce Henry, that she dangled her virginity as bait for him.

Yes, Anne had a hand in the ill-treatment of Catherine and Mary, something that she appears to have regretted in her last days, but she wasn't solely responsible for it, and Henry was very much in charge. No woman ever controlled Henry VIII, he wasn't a puppet. If you think that Anne Boleyn deserved to be beheaded because of Henry's treatment of these women then I really don't know what to say to you.

As for her being responsible for England breaking with Rome, for the executions that took place during the Reformation, for

Mary I turning out the way she did and doing what she did, for Henry's 'tyranny'… Hmmm… I didn't realise that Anne was the one in charge? What else can we blame her for? World poverty?

Just desserts, karma, you reap what you sow, what goes around comes around…

Really?

I despair when I see these types of comments on social media about historical people being executed. Perhaps I should be glad that there are such perfect people in the world who can sit in judgement on those of us who are flawed. I pity people who make these types of comment about Anne Boleyn, I really do, because they have no compassion. I'd like to take them out of their ivory towers and glass houses back in time to Anne Boleyn's trial, to the executions of those five men, to Anne's last days in the Tower, to the nights she spent in prayer, to Anne's execution, to Archbishop Cranmer's garden when he explained to his good friend Alexander Alesius that Anne was being executed that day before being overcome with grief, to the Boleyn family as they heard the news of their children's deaths… "This is real", I'd remind them over and over, "this is not a Game of Thrones episode."

I'm sorry that this is an emotive post and not at all a scholarly article, but sometimes I worry about people, and sometimes it all becomes too much for me, and I have to have my say. I don't believe that Anne Boleyn was an angel, I don't believe that she should be put on a pedestal, I think that she had her flaws and that she wasn't a nice person at times. Like all of us, she had her good points too – she appears to have inspired love and loyalty in those around her, she was charitable and was interested in poor relief and education, she was a patron to religious reformers, she believed in the dissemination of the English Bible, she was courageous, she was witty, she spoke her mind and was true to herself and her beliefs… She was a multi-faceted character, and that's what makes her fascinating to me. Whatever her flaws, though, she didn't deserve her end. It wasn't karma, it wasn't her "just desserts", it wasn't the result of any game she played, it was a travesty and a tragedy. It's something that should make us feel horrified and sick, not satisfied and happy.

Just minutes before she was executed, Anne Boleyn said: "And if any person will meddle of my cause, I require them to judge the best." I choose to do that, and thankfully I'm not alone.

Notes and Sources

"Whoso List to Hunt", poem by Sir Thomas Wyatt the Elder.

Lindsey, Karen (1996) Divorced, Beheaded, Survived: A Feminist Reinterpretation Of The Wives Of Henry VIII, Da Capo Press.

Rumens, Carol (2009) "Poem of the week: Whoso List to Hunt by Thomas Wyatt", The Guardian, Monday 10 August 2009. See https://www.theguardian.com/books/booksblog/2009/aug/10/poem-of-the-week-thomas-wyatt

Wolf Hall and Cardinal Wolsey going down to Hell

Episode 2 of "Wolf Hall", the BBC dramatisation of Hilary Mantel's novel, closed with Cardinal Wolsey's death and Cromwell watching a performance of a court masque in which an actor playing Wolsey is mocked for his low birth and chased off to Beelzebub in Hell by demons. The king and Anne Boleyn laugh and applaud, while it is clear to viewers that Cromwell finds the whole thing shocking and distasteful. He watches as the demons leave the stage and take off their masks: George Boleyn, Henry Norris, Francis Weston and William Brereton.

When a weeping George Cavendish (Wolsey's gentleman-usher) recounts Wolsey's last days and death and tells Cromwell of how he has "prayed to God to send vengeance upon them all", Cromwell quietly assures him "No need to trouble God, George, I'll take it in hand." It is clear that Cromwell is going to take revenge on all those he holds responsible for Wolsey's downfall and all those who mocked his former master. It is a moving scene.

In Mantel's sequel, *Bring Up the Bodies*, after the executions of the men in May 1536, Thomas Wriothesley says to Cromwell: "All the players are gone […] All four who carried the cardinal to Hell; and also the poor fool Mark who made a ballad of their exploits." Cromwell replies: "All four [...] All five."

The masque scene is a dramatic one, particularly as the TV adaptation flicks between the masque, Cromwell being sworn in as a privy councillor, and Cavendish's account of Wolsey's death. The reader/viewer can understand how Cromwell feels. Cromwell has a real motive for bringing down Anne Boleyn, her brother George, Henry Norris, William Brereton and Francis Weston. Wolsey's downfall and this farce explain how those men got caught up in Anne's fall in May 1536 and why they had to die.

But is it true?

Well, yes and no, but mostly no.

Hilary Mantel has taken a real event from 1531 and used it to provide her protagonist with a motive for what she has him plotting a few years later. The farce "Cardinal Wolsey going down to Hell" really did take place, but not as Mantel presents it in her novel or how it is seen on TV.

In reality, the farce was performed at Thomas Boleyn's London home at a private dinner for Claude la Guische, the French ambassador, in January 1531. The aim of the farce was, as historian Greg Walker points out, to stress "the King's new, more hostile attitude towards the Roman Church and all its agents", while "also tacitly reminding the French of their own supposedly 'special relationship' with Wolsey, and their alleged involvement in his plotting immediately prior to his fall." It was an opportunity for Thomas Boleyn, Earl of Wiltshire, and his brother-in-law, Thomas Howard, 3rd Duke of Norfolk, to show the French ambassador their importance and status now that Wolsey was gone. Wolsey's time in power was over, and now France should deal with Wiltshire and Norfolk, was the message. However, according to Eustace Chapuys, the imperial ambassador, their plan backfired, and la Guische was offended by the play and by Norfolk's idea of having it published:

"Some time ago the earl of Vulchier [Wiltshire] invited to supper Monsieur de la Guiche, for whose amusement he caused a farce to be acted of the Cardinal (Wolsey) going down to Hell; for which La Guiche much blamed the Earl, and still more the Duke for his ordering the said farce to be printed. They have been ever since [Jocquin's departure] entertaining the said gentleman most splendidly, and making the most of him on every occasion, and yet I am told that however well treated by them he still says very openly what he thinks of them, and laughs at their eccentricities in matters of government and administration."

Although historian Robert Hutchinson writes that the masque was commissioned by George Boleyn and performed at court at Greenwich Palace, there is no evidence of this. Anne Boleyn's father and uncle were the ones behind the masque, and although it is likely that George was present, there is no evidence that he or any of the men caught up in Anne's fall in 1536, played any parts in it. As Clare Cherry and I said in a previous article on *Bring Up the Bodies*, "the notion of an aspiring courtier, diplomat and politician demeaning himself by performing in a farce is… farcical!" and there is no mention of Norris, Brereton, Weston and Smeaton even attending the performance. While the scene provides Cromwell with a motive and builds empathy and sympathy, it does not tell the real story.

Who was ultimately responsible for Anne Boleyn's fall and why these men were caught up in it are questions that are still being debated today. Did Cromwell plot against Anne Boleyn of his own accord or was he simply following orders from the king? Why did Norris, Weston, Brereton, Smeaton and George Boleyn have to fall? Were they in Cromwell's way? Were they just innocent scapegoats? The answers to these questions are not clear, but Norris, Weston, Brereton and Smeaton had nothing whatsoever to do with Wolsey's fall, and Cromwell had no need to seek revenge on them.

Mantel's Cromwell and his motivations may make for good fiction and TV but her story is a fictional one, and her Cromwell is far removed from that of the historical sources.

Notes and Sources

Wolf Hall, BBC2 adaptation, Episode 2: Entirely Beloved, aired 28 January 2015

Mantel, Hilary (2012) *Bring Up the Bodies*, Fourth Estate, London, p.400

Walker, Greg (2008) *Plays of Persuasion: Drama and Politics at the Court of Henry VIII*, p.20, Cambridge University Press, p.20

Calendar of State Papers, Spain, Volume 4 Part 2, 1531-1533, ed. Pascual de Gayangos (London, 1882), British History Online http://www.british-history.ac.uk/cal-state-papers/spain/vol4/no2 [accessed 18 January 2019]

Hutchinson, Robert (2009) *House of Treason: The Rise and Fall of a Tudor Dynasty*, Orion

Bring Up the Bodies: Fact versus Fiction – https://www.theanneboleynfiles.com/bring-up-bodies-fact-versus-fiction/

Was Anne Boleyn in love with Henry Norris?

First off, before I go into this topic in detail, I have to post a disclaimer. I have to say that there is no way that I can answer that question definitively. I have not found a letter or journal where Anne or Norris share their personal feelings for each other, and I just cannot say one way or the other for sure. What I can do is explain why one author has concluded that Anne may well have loved Norris, and then explain why I don't give credence to the idea.

The theory

In the author's note section of her novel *Anne Boleyn: A King's Obsession*, Alison Weir writes of "the unacknowledged – until near the end – attraction between Anne and Norris" and goes on to explain that "this was suggested by the wording of her last confession. From her insistence that 'she had never offended with her body' against the King, it might be inferred that she had offended in her heart or her thoughts, and that she secretly loved another but had never gone so far as to consummate that love." Weir states that "of the men accused with her, Norris was the likeliest of her affections." Weir then says that her theory, is just that, a theory, but that it's "a compelling one" because we know that Norris did confess to something that he later retracted.

Weir is not saying Anne and Norris were definitely in love, but she's putting the idea forward as a "compelling" theory. It's not a new theory; Weir says the same in her earlier non-fiction book *The Lady in the Tower*.

The evidence

In *The Lady in the Tower*, Alison Weir quotes Eustace Chapuys, the imperial ambassador, citing the Letters and Papers of Henry VIII's reign, Chapuys records that he had heard from one of the ladies attending Anne Boleyn in the Tower that "before and after receiving the Sacrament, [Anne] affirmed to her, on the damnation of her soul, that she had never offended with her body against the King." This record can indeed be found in Letters and Papers, in a letter written by Chapuys to Emperor Charles V on 19th May 1536. It has been translated from French.

It also appears in the Calendar of State Papers, Spain, with a slightly different translation:

"The lady in whose keeping she has been sends me word, in great secrecy, that before and after her receiving the Holy Sacrament, she affirmed, on peril of her soul's damnation, that she had not misconducted herself so far as her husband the King was concerned."

There, the editor notes that the dispatch was originally in French and "Mostly in cipher". The original French is also given:

"La dame qui la eu en garde, ma envoye dire en grant secret que la dicte concubiuc, auant et apres la reception du sainct sacrament, luy a affirme sur la dampnation de son ame quelle ne sestait meffaicte de son corps envers ce roy."

The key words are "quelle ne sestait meffaicte de son corps envers ce roy." Historian and academic G. W. Bernard has translated these as "she had not misused herself with her body towards the king", and that seems a more accurate translation to me.

The other piece of evidence Alison Weir uses to back up her theory is the story of Sir Henry Norris's retracted confession. Norris's servant, George Constantine, wrote of how Norris's chaplain told him that Norris had confessed after being taken to the Tower of London but that when this confession was laid before him at his trial, Norris stated that "he was deceaved to do the same by the Erle of Hampton that now ys." Constantine is referring to Sir William Fitzwilliam, Treasurer of the King's Household.

The challenge

Now it's time for me to challenge this theory.

First, let's handle Norris's alleged confession as recorded by George Constantine. Although Constantine mentions this retracted confession, he also writes of the king examining Norris on their ride back from the May Day joust and how Norris "wold confess no thinge to the Kynge" even though the king promised him a pardon "in case he wolde utter the trewth." We also know that Norris pleaded innocent at his trial and that he claimed to have been deceived when Fitzwilliam interrogated him. Constantine does not give any more details. Other sources make no mention of Norris confessing, mentioning only Mark Smeaton's confession, and Sir Edward Baynton was concerned about this, writing in a letter to Fitzwilliam:

> "this shallbe to advertyse yow that here is myche communycacion that noman will confesse any thynge agaynst her, but allonly Marke of any actuell thynge. Wherefore (in my folishe conceyte) it shulde myche toche the King's honor if it shulde no farther appeere. And I cannot beleve but that the other two bee as…culpapull as ever was hee."

Baynton is clearly saying here that only Mark has confessed

to anything.

Historian Eric Ives - in his notes on Norris withdrawing the statement he made to Fitzwilliam - makes the point that Norris may have been confessing to his conversation with Anne (the one regarding "dead men's shoes"), "but denied the implication", i.e. that they were plotting against the king. Ives also cites a letter from Sir William Kingston, Constable of the Tower of London, which is badly mutilated but mentions Kingston sending a knave to Norris in the Tower. It reads "he assured hym agayn ....ay thyng of my confession he ys worthye to have ..... hyt I defy hym;" which Ives believes "can be reconstructed as '[whoever tries to take advantage of] anything of my confession, he is worthy to have [my place here; and if he stand to] it, I defy him.'" which makes sense.

It's impossible to know exactly what happened when Norris was taken to the Tower, what was said, what he allegedly confessed and how he was deceived, but he retracted whatever was said and pleaded innocent. This story cannot, I feel, be used as evidence that Norris was in love with Anne or vice versa.

But the main point I'd like to make here is regarding Anne's words when she swore on the sacrament. I am of the opinion that it's quite a leap to take someone saying that they had not offended the king with their body to mean that they *had* offended him with their heart or mind.

Anne had been accused of offending the king with *her body*. She had been accused of committing adultery with five men; those were offences concerning physical actions using the body. It stands to reason, therefore, that she would answer that accusation and deny it. Her oath on the sacrament makes perfect sense; she is swearing her innocence.

If we are to read anything further into her words, and I don't like doing so, then it makes more sense with what we know of Anne, her behaviour and other things that she said, that she would be suggesting that she had offended the king with her words. At their fall in 1536, it was said that Anne Boleyn and her brother,

George, had made fun of ballads that the king had composed and that Anne had discussed the king's sexual problems with her sister-in-law, Jane. Lancelot de Carles, secretary to the French ambassador, wrote a poem about Anne Boleyn's life and death. In it, he recorded a speech Anne made at her trial, quoting her as saying that she had not always given the king the "deference" and "humility" that he deserved and that she had shown jealousy, adding "In this I know that I lacked virtue". De Carles has her admitting that she had offended the king in this way.

We also know that Anne's relationship with the king was volatile, one that saw them "merry" one minute and then arguing the next. Their marriage was a real one based on love and passion, and that, of course, led to disagreements and cross words being spoken. Anne also showed jealousy when she noticed the king showing interest in other ladies at court. She even tried to get a particular lady removed from court in 1534. Anne probably did offend the king with her words and was not as submissive as a queen consort perhaps should have been.

At her trial on 15th May 1536, Anne gave a spirited defence. Chronicler Charles Wriothesley recorded that after her indictment was read out, Anne "made so wise and discreet aunsweres to all thinges layde against her, excusing herselfe with her wordes so clearlie, as thoughe she had never bene faultie to the same." She argued her innocence. In Lancelot de Carles' account of her speech at her trial, Anne states that she has "always been faithful to the King". While admitting to jealousy, not showing him the deference he deserved, she states:

> "But for the rest of it, God knows
> That my wrongdoings did not go beyond this:
> And I will certainly not confess more."

I'm sure that being in love with another man would have been a "wrongdoing".

Anne Boleyn was also a woman that knew her Bible. She was a woman with a keen interest in religious reform, a woman who encouraged the publication of the Bible in English and who read texts about how the Church should be focusing on the authority of Scripture. Anne owned a copy of William Tyndale's translation of the New Testament, in which can be found these words:

> "Ye haue hearde howe it was sayde to the of olde tyme: Thou shalt not comitt advoutrie. But I say vnto you that whosoeuer looketh on a wyfe lustynge after her hathe comitted advoutrie with hir alredy in his hert." Matthew 5: 27-28.

Here, Jesus is saying that a person who lusts after someone who is married has already committed adultery even if they have not had sexual relations. Anne was married, for her to have been in love with or to have had lustful thoughts about another man would have constituted adultery in the mind of someone who believed in the authority of scriptures, as Anne did. I doubt that she would have felt that she could claim to be innocent if she had truly been in love with one of her husband's best friends.

Another point is that we don't actually know what Anne said when she swore her innocence on the sacrament on that May day in 1536. Chapuys writes that one of her ladies told him, so that's second-hand information, and we don't know whether Anne's words were paraphrased rather than quoted accurately. Sir William Kingston's report to Thomas Cromwell on 18th May 1536, which is about Anne sending for him to witness her taking the sacrament, is damaged and all we can read is:

> "she sent for me that I myght be with hyr at [soche tyme] asshe reysayved the gud lord to the in tent I shuld here hy[r speke as] towchyng her innosensy alway to be clere."

So no details of her words but it appears that she was swearing to her innocence.

My final point is that there is nothing linking Anne Boleyn and Henry Norris romantically before Anne's fall. On 29th April

1536, three days before her arrest, it is reported that Anne had an altercation with Norris. At this time, Norris, a widower, was courting Anne's cousin, Madge Shelton. Anne is said to have asked Norris why he was taking so long in marrying her cousin, and when he replied that he "would tarry a time" she rebuked him, saying, "You look for dead men's shoes, for if aught came to the King but good, you would look to have me", thus accusing Norris of delaying his marriage to Madge because he fancied her. A horrified Norris replied that "if he [should have any such thought] he would his head were off." This exchange started as a game of courtly love, where a knight was meant to woo his queen and be a little in love with her, but ended up with Anne speaking recklessly of the king's death, something which could be construed as treason. A game of courtly love gone too far, not a romantic exchange by any stretch of the imagination and certainly not proof that they were in love. Norris was courting Anne's cousin, and Anne seems to want him to get his act together and marry her soon. I can't see this conversation as two sweethearts flirting.

Did Anne Boleyn love Sir Henry Norris?

Who knows? It's impossible to say. However, I don't find it a compelling theory. I think Anne Boleyn and Henry Norris were completely innocent, and that noble Norris went to his death rather than confess to something that he didn't do.

Notes and Sources

Weir, Alison (2017) *Six Tudor Queens: Anne Boleyn: A King's Obsession*, taken from "Author's Note", p.511 in an ARC.

Weir, Alison (2009) *The Lady in the Tower: The Fall of Anne Boleyn*, Jonathan Cape, p. 252. Weir says "Nonetheless the wording of her confession is interesting. It may be that she merely wished to emphasise that she had been faithful to the King, but from her insistence that 'she had never offended with her body against him, it might be inferred that she had offended in other ways, perhaps with her heart or her thoughts, and that she had perhaps secretly loved another, possibly Norris, but had never gone so far as to consummate that love."

'Henry VIII: May 1536, 16-20', in Letters and Papers, Foreign and Domestic, Henry VIII, Volume 10, January-June 1536, ed. James Gairdner (London, 1887), pp. 371-391. British History Online http://www.british-history.ac.uk/letters-papers-hen8/vol10/pp371-391

'Spain: May 1536, 16-31', in Calendar of State Papers, Spain, Volume 5 Part 2, 1536-1538, ed. Pascual de Gayangos (London, 1888), pp. 118-133. British History Online http:// www.british-history.ac.uk/cal-state-papers/spain/vol5/no2/ pp118-133. See also Note 26 on that page.

Bernard, G. W. (2010) *Anne Boleyn: Fatal Attractions*, Yale University Press, p. 172.

Archaeologia: Or Miscellaneous Tracts Relating to Antiquity, Published by the Society of Antiquities, Volume XXIII (1831) p. 64.

ed. Ellis, Sir Henry (1825) *Original letters, illustrative of English history...*, Volume II, p. 61.

Ives, Eric (2004, 2005) *The Life and Death of Anne Boleyn*, Blackwell Publishing, p. 420.

Cavendish, George (1825) *The Life of Cardinal Wolsey and Metrical Visions* from the Original Autograph Manuscript, Samuel Weller Singer, p. 223.

Lancelot de Carles' poem "De la Royne d'Angleterre" is from Ascoli, Georges, La Grande-Bretagne Devant L'opinion Française Depuis La Guerre de Cent Ans Jusqu'à La Fin Du XVIe Siècle, my translation was done at my request by Paolo Dagonnier.

'Henry VIII: October 1534, 11-15', in Letters and Papers, Foreign and Domestic, Henry VIII, Volume 7, 1534, ed. James Gairdner (London, 1883), pp. 482-487. British

History Online http://www.british-history.ac.uk/letters-papers-hen8/vol7/pp482-487

Wriothesley, Charles (1875) *A Chronicle of England During the Reigns of the Tudors, from A.D. 1485 to 1559*, Volume I, p. 37-38.

'Henry VIII: May 1536, 1-10', in Letters and Papers, Foreign and Domestic, Henry VIII, Volume 10, January-June 1536, ed. James Gairdner (London, 1887), pp. 329-349. British History Online http://www.british-history.ac.uk/letters-papers-hen8/vol10/pp329-349

Anne Boleyn and George Boleyn

On 2nd May 1536, Queen Anne Boleyn was arrested at Greenwich Palace and her brother, George Boleyn, Lord Rochford, was arrested at Whitehall. They were both taken to the Tower of London and imprisoned there. On 15th May 1536, they were tried one after the other in the King's Hall of the royal palace at the Tower. The siblings were tried by a jury of their peers, presided over by their uncle, Thomas Howard, 3rd Duke of Norfolk, as Lord High Steward. They were charged with high treason, found guilty and condemned to death.

Anne was accused of seducing and committing adultery with five men and conspiring with them to kill the king; one of them was her own brother, George. The indictment drawn up by the Grand Jury of Middlesex stated that Anne was seduced by evil, had malice in her heart, and had frail and carnal appetites, and said that:

> "The Queen, on 2 Nov. of the 27th year of Henry VIII's reign and several times before and after, at Westminster, procured and incited her own natural brother, Geo. Boleyn, lord Rocheford, gentleman of the privy chamber, to violate her, alluring him with her tongue in the said George's mouth, and the said George's tongue in hers, and also with kisses,

presents, and jewels; whereby he, despising the commands of God, and all human laws, on 5 Nov. the 27th year of Henry VIII's reign, violated and carnally knew the said Queen, his own sister, at Westminster; which he also did on divers other days before and after at the same place, sometimes by his own procurement and sometimes by the Queen's."

So, they were accused of committing incest, and in quite salacious detail – that language would surely have shocked those listening in court.

Both defended themselves admirably. George defended himself so well that it was reported "that several of those present wagered 10 to 1 that he would be acquitted", but it didn't make any difference and the other four men had been found guilty anyway, so there was no way out for the Boleyns.

But what evidence did the Crown use to accuse Anne and George of incest?

Well, some have said that Jane Boleyn, wife of George Boleyn, was responsible for providing the Crown with evidence of incest. However, that idea is based on a later fictional account of her scaffold speech, which is not corroborated by the eye witness account of her execution or by other contemporary sources. Jane did not confess to bringing the Boleyn siblings down. Jane is also not named as providing evidence in 1536, the only names mentioned as providing information are the Countess of Worcester, Lady Bridget Wingfield, Nan Cobham and a mystery "one maid more", who Eric Ives believes to have been Margery Horsman.

Elizabeth Browne, Countess of Worcester, was named as the first accuser in a letter written by John Hussee, servant of Lord and Lady Lisle. Lancelot de Carles, secretary to the French ambassador in London, also named her in his poem on Anne Boleyn, writing that when her brother Anthony Browne accused her of loose behaviour, the countess defended herself by saying that she was no worse than the Queen who had offended with musician Mark Smeaton and her own brother. As Eric Ives has pointed out in his biography of Anne, this was probably an exaggeration, and the countess was probably just saying that she was no more a flirt than the queen. Justice John Spelman, who wrote a report on the trial, makes no mention of the Countess, so her information obviously wasn't that important, and she certainly did not get called as a witness.

Justice Spelman's assessment of the trial was that "all the evidence was of bawdry and lechery, so there was no such whore in the realm", which makes it sound like everything was grossly exaggerated. Eustace Chapuys, the imperial ambassador and a man who was no friend of the Boleyns, states that no witnesses were called and that no proof of George's guilt "was produced except that of his having once passed many hours in her company, and other little follies." Chapuys also noted that although Mark Smeaton had confessed to sleeping with the queen, the others "were sentenced on mere presumption or on very slight grounds, without legal proof or valid confession". He was very skeptical of the charges.

But could there by any truth to the incest charge?

Could Anne Boleyn have been so desperate to provide the king with a son that she'd sleep with her brother to try and conceive?

No and no.

Nobody before May 1536 had ever commented on the siblings' relationship being unnatural in any way. There wasn't any gossip, no accusations, nothing. Anne and George were very close. George commissioned a beautiful illuminated manuscript, a translation of a religious work, for his sister, and wrote a beautiful dedication to her, referring to himself as her "most loving and friendly brother". It was a beautiful gift and is evidence of the siblings' affection and respect for each other and their shared reformed faith. However, there is absolutely nothing "dodgy" or weird in the dedication or their behaviour to each other. A close bond does not equal a sexual relationship.

We know from George's trial that Anne had confided in George's wife, Jane, that the king was having problems with impotence. Now, if the king was having sexual problems, it just doesn't make sense to me that Anne would sleep with her brother to help her conceive. The king would surely know that the baby couldn't be his. And I don't see it as a natural step. "Oh, the king can't get me pregnant, and I really need to give him a prince of Wales, hey George, how about it?"! No, just no.

What about the deformed foetus that Anne miscarried in 1536. That has been used in fiction to back up the idea of incest – a monstrous baby from a monstrous act. But there wasn't a deformed foetus! No contemporary report makes any mention of there being something wrong with the foetus that Anne miscarried in January 1536, that idea comes from a much later account, in the 1580s, written in a work of Catholic propaganda that also stated that Anne had an extra finger, a projecting tooth, a wen and that she'd been sent to France after sleeping with her father's butler and chaplain.

Anne and George were both pious people. They were interested in theology; they were interested in reform of the church, the authority of scripture, the translation of the Bible into English etc. To suggest that they would have had no problem committing incest, something which would have been considered evil and monstrous, makes no sense at all.

The charges against Anne Boleyn, George Boleyn and the other four men did and do not make sense. Eric Ives pointed out that three-quarters of the alleged offences can be dismissed, and would be in today's court of law, because either Anne, or the man she was alleged to have slept with, was not at the palace in question on the date cited in the indictments. It was all very careless, but that doesn't matter when a jury knows what is expected of them.

I am of the opinion that the incest charge was added to completely blacken the Boleyn name. Adultery was pretty good, but incest was nasty, it was completely scandalous and would be remembered. Anne was willing to stop at nothing to satisfy her carnal cravings. She was a monster and the king was a victim. That was the Anne that needed to be portrayed to bring her down once and for all.

Notes and Sources

Wriothesley, Charles. *A Chronicle of England During the Reigns of the Tudors, from A.D. 1485 to 1559*, Appendix, Baga de Secretis Pouch VIII, p. 201.

'Henry VIII: May 1536, 16-20', in Letters and Papers, Foreign and Domestic, Henry VIII, Volume 10, January-June 1536, ed. James Gairdner (London, 1887), pp. 371-391. British History Online http://www.british-history.ac.uk/letters-papers-hen8/vol10/pp371-391.

ed. St Clare Byrne, Muriel (1981) The Lisle Letters, Volume 3, The University of Chicago Press, p. 377, letter 703a, John Husee to Lady Lisle, 24 May 1536.

de Carles, Lancelot, "Poème sur la Mort d'Anne Boleyn", lines 861-864, in *La Grande Bretagne devant L'Opinion Française depuis la Guerre de Cent Ans jusqu'a la Fin du XVI Siècle*, George Ascoli

ed. Baker, J.H. (1977) *The Reports of Sir John Spelman*, Selden Society, London, pp. 70-71.

Ives, Eric (2004) *The Life and Death of Anne Boleyn*, Wiley-Blackwell.

The Fall of Anne Boleyn – why did it happen?

This article is based on a talk that I gave to a tour group at Hever Castle. I gave it on 12th May 2019, on the anniversary of the trials of four men at a special commission of oyer and terminer in Westminster Hall, London, in 1536.

On 12th May 1536, groom of the stool, Sir Henry Norris; royal favourite, Sir Francis Weston; royal favourite and powerful man, William Brereton, and court musician Mark Smeaton were all found guilty of high treason for having had sexual relations with Queen Anne Boleyn and plotting to kill the king. They were all sentenced to death, to be hanged, drawn and quartered at Tyburn, although this sentence was later commuted to the more merciful death by beheading.

This was a hugely important moment because there was no going back from here. If these men were guilty, then so was Queen Anne.

Queen Anne Boleyn's fall was super fast, much faster than that of her cousin, Queen Catherine Howard, which was three months from the start of the investigations in November 1541 to Catherine's execution in February 1542. Anne Boleyn died less than a month after the investigation into her conduct began. In

1541, in Catherine's case, many people were investigated and interrogated, and many of them were interrogated several times, yet there were hardly any interrogations in 1536. I've been researching Catherine's fall for a few years now, on and off, and there are records of the interrogations - you have the likes of Mary Hall, Henry Mannox and Francis Dereham being interrogated, members of the queen's household being questioned, the Howards and Tilneys being tried for misprision of treason for hiding Catherine's past, Jane Boleyn being tried for treason for helping Catherine…. Lots of people being questioned and subsequently tried. But how many were interrogated in 1536? Not many, and not one of Anne's ladies got into trouble, yet the queen was never alone, a lady slept with her in the same room on a pallet bed. How could Anne have had all of those affairs without help from a trusted lady or two?

They were very different falls, and if I had to say why *I* think they're different, then I'd say because Catherine's was a **real** investigation, while Anne's was a set-up.

In 1541, Archbishop Thomas Cranmer was informed of allegations regarding Catherine's past, he passed this information on to the king, and then the king ordered an investigation to be launched. It was a thorough and time-consuming investigation, which had various stages as more information came to light, and more and more people became involved. It was real, and the king was to be devastated by the results of it.

But why did Anne Boleyn get executed in 1536?

Well, it was not karma! I see so many comments on social media about Anne being a usurper, about her deserving her end for treating Catherine and Mary badly, even for being a religious terrorist, which is a weird one! Or comments regarding her being overly ambitious, for playing a game and losing, for climbing too high….. The whole "pride comes before a fall" idea.

But what happened? How could a woman go from being the love of someone's life to being beheaded? Why was she set up?

How could she go from being relentlessly pursued and hunted down, from being bombarded with love letters, to ending her life on the scaffold as a traitor and having her name blackened for eternity?

It's so hard to understand.

King Henry VIII courted Anne for at least six years before their marriage. He moved heaven and earth to be with her, he went through the Great Matter, and he broke with Rome. He and Cromwell instituted all kinds of legal measures, acts and oaths, and these measures had a huge impact – people were executed, including men like Sir Thomas More who had been nothing but loyal to the king, Henry's wife and daughter were banished and separated, Henry upset friends and fellow rulers alike, he upset the pope, and he put England at risk. All that, and then Anne was only his queen for three years.

Anne's rise was dramatic, and so was her fall, and it wasn't down to one single factor. There are various factors in Anne Boleyn's fall, and we could describe it as a perfect storm, with everything coming together at once. Let's consider some of the factors, and also the theories, regarding her fall.

Thomas Cromwell

Some people believe that Anne Boleyn's fall was solely down to Thomas Cromwell, Henry VIII's chief advisor and right-hand man.

Cromwell and Anne had fallen out over the dissolution of monasteries and where the proceeds were going. As monasteries were being dissolved, the wealth was going straight into the king's coffers, whereas Anne felt that it could be put to better use and used for educational and charitable causes. In April 1536, Anne launched an attack on Cromwell through her almoner John Skips's sermon, where Anne was Queen Esther saving the people from her husband, the king, who had been given wicked advice by his advisor, Haman, who, of course, represented Thomas Cromwell.

Anne was also an obstacle to Cromwell's foreign policy plans. Anne was pro-French, whereas Cromwell was keen on an imperial alliance. He obviously would have been concerned about Anne's stance and her influence.

Back in 1535, according to Eustace Chapuys, Anne had even threatened Cromwell's life saying that she'd like to see his head off his shoulders! However, Cromwell had not seemed at all worried about this threat.

When I look at the events of 1536, I see Cromwell as the king's loyal servant. I believe that the mechanics of Anne's fall were down to Cromwell, but I see him as simply turning the king's dreams into reality, getting rid of a wife that the king doesn't want any more. It would have been far too risky for Cromwell to have moved against the queen without the king's support. I also think that if it had solely been down to Cromwell, then, as historian John Schofield as pointed out, it would have been a far more watertight case, rather than the mess it was. And the incest charge smacks of personal revenge to me.

Henry VIII

As I say, I believe that Henry VIII wanted rid of his second wife, and he asked Cromwell to do it, and to do it at any cost. The king needed Anne's fall to be final; he couldn't afford Anne to be in the wings and to be a thorn in his side like Catherine of Aragon had been for many years. Anne needed to be gone completely, and to be gone forever.

But why the need to get rid of Anne?

I see several reasons:

Henry VIII's jousting accident – The king had suffered an accident while jousting on 24th January 1536. While I don't believe that this caused any serious injury, as the English sources do not support this, I do believe that it served as a stark reminder of the king's mortality and his need for a son to succeed him. He had an illegitimate son and two daughters, he really needed an heir and a spare, and he wasn't getting any younger.

Anne's miscarriage – Just five days after the king's jousting accident, Anne miscarried a male foetus. She'd been pregnant three times but hadn't provided the king with a son. The miscarriage was a huge blow to Henry, and he was said to have commented: "I see that God will not give me male children." Did he believe that history was repeating itself and that this marriage was like his first, i.e. contrary to God's wishes? Possibly. The lack of a son could well have made him believe that God was not blessing this anointed sovereign because there was something wrong.

Jane Seymour – Henry VIII had started a flirtation with one of his wife's maids of honour, a woman by the name of Jane Seymour, by at least January 1536. Jane was a few years younger than Anne and came from a large family with lots of sons. She was also the polar opposite of Anne, being fair, meek and mild, and submissive, and not at all feisty or argumentative. She must have been a breath of fresh air, a welcome change, and she was also telling him just how unpopular his second marriage was with his people, how wrong it was, and backing up all his fears and stoking his paranoia. Henry wanted Jane and the opportunity of having sons with her; Anne had to go.

Henry's sexual problems – By 1536, the king was experiencing sexual problems. It appears that he was suffering from erectile dysfunction, and, of course, this had to be his wife's fault. He was, after all, God's anointed sovereign. He must have been humiliated, particularly as Anne had confided in her sister-in-law, Jane Boleyn, who had passed the gossip on to her husband, George Boleyn. His manhood was being challenged, and he'd also heard that Anne and George were making fun of him and laughing at the poetry he'd written and his fashion sense. He was becoming a laughing stock to his wife, the woman he'd raised from maid of honour to queen.

A sense of betrayal – Henry VIII had done everything to possess Anne. He had raised her from maid of honour to queen at such a cost to himself and his country, and she had not given him a son. She had let him down.

A fizzling out of love and passion – Henry and Anne's relationship had been a love match. Henry had pursued Anne because he was obsessed with her; he was passionately in love with her. Their relationship was based on love and passion, rather than on diplomacy. An arranged marriage could be rather cold to start with, but could turn into one of respect and friendship, and even love, but Henry's second marriage had started off passionately. The pressure of the long courtship, the opposition the couple encountered at every turn, the Great Matter, the loss of his friends, and everything that had happened may well have sapped the life, passion and love out of the marriage. Love had turned to resentment, and Anne was a difficult character. The relationship of sunshine and showers had turned to sunshine and storms, and more and more storms. Anne felt threatened by other women who caught the king's eye because that's how her relationship with the king had started. She was jealous of Henry's flirtations because they were a threat to her. Perhaps Henry felt that Anne was too much work, and he was tired. The passion fizzled out and was replaced by resentment, and this, in turn, turned to hate. Henry had fallen in love with Anne for who she was, a very different kind of woman, but perhaps he fell out of love with her for the very same reason.

Anne was getting in the way politically. Catherine of Aragon was now gone, and Henry had celebrated her death in January 1536 by saying "God be praised that we are free from all suspicion of war!". Catherine had been Emperor Charles V's aunt, and her opposition to the annulment of her marriage to Henry VIII had made the king's political life very difficult. The situation with her had prevented an alliance with the Empire. Her death meant that Henry had no argument with the emperor any more, but the pro-French Anne wanted the king to ally with France, not the Empire. If Anne could be removed, then the king could ally with anyone.

Catherine of Aragon was dead, so now he could set Anne

aside without being forced to go back to his first wife.

I think that Henry VIII's actions and behaviour in 1536 are evidence of his role in Anne's fall as the instigator. There was a significant difference in the king's behaviour in 1536 and 1541, the falls of his second and fifth wife.

In 1541, Charles de Marillac, the French ambassador, reported Henry's reaction when he was presented with the evidence gathered against his fifth wife, Catherine Howard:

> "This King has changed his love for the Queen into hatred, and taken such grief at being deceived that of late it was thought he had gone mad, for he called for a sword to slay her he had loved so much. Sitting in Council he suddenly called for horses without saying where he would go. Sometimes he said irrelevantly that that wicked woman had never such delight in her incontinency as she should have torture in her death. And finally he took to tears regretting his ill luck in meeting with such ill-conditioned wives, and blaming his Council for this last mischief. The ministers have done their best to make him forget his grief, and he is gone 25 miles from here with no company but musicians and ministers of pastime."

Eustace Chapuys, the imperial ambassador, reported that "this king has wonderfully felt the case of the Queen, his wife, and that he has certainly shown greater sorrow and regret at her loss than at the faults, loss, or divorce of his preceding wives."

Henry was furious and grief-stricken in 1541. He even wept in front of privy council. Yet in 1536, he was reported as gallivanting with ladies each night while his wife was in prison. His wife had allegedly betrayed him with one of his best friends (Sir Henry Norris, Groom of the Stool), two men he had supported financially (Weston and Smeaton), and her own brother, yet the only sign of any distress at all is when he broke down in tears in front of Henry Fitzroy, his illegitimate son, and claimed that Anne had planned to poison him and his half-sister,

Mary.

Chapuys certainly found the King's behaviour odd:

> "You never saw prince nor man who made greater show
> of his [cuckold's] horns or bore them more pleasantly. I leave
> you to imagine the cause."

Henry knew Anne wasn't guilty, hence his lack of grief and disbelief. He'd already moved on in his heart and mind to Jane Seymour. He even became betrothed to Jane the day after Anne's execution!

Cromwell and the men of 1536

But even if Henry wanted Anne gone so he could move on to Jane and have a son, what about the men? Why did they have to die?

This is where I see Thomas Cromwell's part in the plot. I think the king had ordered him to get rid of Anne at any cost, so Cromwell used this to get rid of obstacles. Like Cardinal Wolsey had used the Eltham Ordnances of 1526 to purge Henry VIII's privy chamber of men he didn't like and who were too influential, Cromwell used Anne Boleyn's fall to get rid of problem men.

William Brereton was opposing Cromwell's proposed reforms in North Wales, and Sir Henry Norris, as groom of the stool and the king's close friend, was too intimate and influential with the king. Groom of the Stool was a very important position as the holder controlled access to the king and people would use him to intercede with the king and pass on petitions. Sir Francis Weston was too close to the king, as was George Boleyn, who would also stick up for his sister and cause problems if he wasn't apprehended too. Then Mark Smeaton, with his lowly status, was the perfect easy target to put pressure on. He could be coerced into providing a false confession.

Jane Seymour

Jane Seymour has to take some responsibility for what happened to Anne Boleyn, along with Sir Nicholas Carew and his group.

On 1ˢᵗ April 1536, Chapuys wrote:

> "The said Marchioness has sent to me to say that by this the King's love and desire towards the said lady was wonderfully increased, and that he had said she had behaved most virtuously, and to show her that he only loved her honorably, he did not intend henceforth to speak with her except in presence of some of her kin; for which reason the King has caused Cromwell to remove from a chamber to which the King can go by certain galleries without being perceived, and has lodged there the eldest brother of the said lady with his wife, in order to bring thither the same young lady, who has been well taught for the most part by those intimate with the King, who hate the concubine, that she must by no means comply with the King's wishes except by way of marriage; in which she is quite firm. She is also advised to tell the King boldly how his marriage is detested by the people, and none consider it lawful..."

Then, on 29ᵗʰ April, he recorded:

> "it will not be Carew's fault if the aforesaid concubine, though a cousin of his, is not overthrown (desarçonee) one of these days, for I hear that he is daily conspiring against her, and trying to persuade Miss Seymour and her friends to accomplish her ruin."

So, it is clear that Jane was being coached in how to behave, what to do, and what to say. She'd learned what had worked with Anne, that saying "no" seemed to make Henry even more determined to have you, and that refusing to be his mistress could lead to a marriage proposal. She had Anne's example to follow. As I said earlier, she was also affirming the king's fears and paranoia about Anne and his marriage.

Now, I can't paint Jane as a wicked usurper, as a homewrecker, because we don't know how much choice she had in the matter, how much of a pawn she was and how much pressure she was under, plus, she had absolutely no way of knowing that her actions could lead to Anne's death. However, she did play her part in bringing Anne down.

A perfect storm

Anne's fall was a perfect storm of factors:
- Catherine of Aragon had died so Henry could move on from Anne without anyone forcing him to return to his first wife.
- Anne had suffered a miscarriage.
- Anne was a diplomatic pain.
- Henry was tired of Anne and was attracted to Jane.
- The Catholic conservatives wanted Anne out of the way and felt that Jane would support their cause and that of Henry's daughter, Mary.
- Anne and Thomas Cromwell were at odds.
- Cromwell wanted rid of some men at court.

It was time for Anne to go.

Notes and Sources

In June 1535, Chapuys recorded: "Cremuel said lately to me that were the Lady to know the familiar terms on which he and I are, she would surely try to cause us both some annoyance, and that only three days ago she and he had had words together, the Lady telling him, among other things, that she would like to see his head off his shoulders. "But," added Cromwell, "I trust so much on my master, that I fancy she cannot do me any harm." I cannot tell whether this is an invention of Cromwell in order to enhance his merchandise. All I can say is, that everyone here considers him Anne's right hand, as I myself told him some time ago. Indeed, I hear from a reliable source that day and night is the Lady working to bring about the duke of Norfolk's disgrace with the King; whether it be owing to his having spoken too freely about her, or because Cromwell, wishes to bring down the aristocracy of this kingdom, and is about to begin by him, I cannot say." Spain: June 1535, 1-15', in Calendar of State Papers, Spain, Volume 5 Part 1, 1534-1535, ed. Pascual de Gayangos (London, 1886), pp. 475-491. British History Online http://www.british-history.ac.uk/cal-state-papers/spain/vol5/no1/pp475-491.

Schofield, John (2008) *The Rise & Fall of Thomas Cromwell: Henry VIII's Most Faithful Servant*, The History Press.

'Spain: February 1536, 21-29', in Calendar of State Papers, Spain, Volume 5 Part 2, 1536-1538, ed. Pascual de Gayangos (London, 1888), pp. 52-66. British History Online http://www.british-history.ac.uk/cal-state-papers/spain/vol5/no2/pp52-66.

'Henry VIII: January 1536, 21-25', in Letters and Papers, Foreign and Domestic, Henry VIII, Volume 10, January-June 1536, ed. James Gairdner (London, 1887), pp. 47-64. British History Online http://www.british-history.ac.uk/letters-papers-hen8/vol10/pp47-64.

'Henry VIII: December 1541, 6-10', in Letters and Papers, Foreign and Domestic, Henry VIII, Volume 16, 1540-1541, ed. James Gairdner and R H Brodie (London, 1898), pp. 660-671. British History Online http://www.british-history.ac.uk/letters-papers-hen8/vol16/pp660-671.

'Spain: December 1541, 1-20', in Calendar of State Papers, Spain, Volume 6 Part 1, 1538-1542, ed. Pascual de Gayangos (London, 1890), pp. 406-425. British History Online http://www.british-history.ac.uk/cal-state-papers/spain/vol6/no1/pp406-425.

'Henry VIII: April 1536, 1-10', in Letters and Papers, Foreign and Domestic, Henry VIII, Volume 10, January-June 1536, ed. James Gairdner (London, 1887), pp. 240-259. British History Online http://www.british-history.ac.uk/letters-papers-hen8/vol10/pp240-259.

'Henry VIII: April 1536, 26-30', in Letters and Papers, Foreign and Domestic, Henry VIII, Volume 10, January-June 1536, ed. James Gairdner (London, 1887), pp. 310-329. British History Online http://www.british-history.ac.uk/letters-papers-hen8/vol10/pp310-329.

Ridgway, Claire (2012) *The Fall of Anne Boleyn: A Countdown*, MadeGlobal Publishing.

Ives, Eric (2004) *The Life and Death of Anne Boleyn*, Wiley-Blackwell.

The other victims of 1536

This article is based on a talk I did for the Anne Boleyn Experience Tour in 2018. The tour focused on Queen Anne Boleyn, and rightly so. She is a fascinating historical figure, a woman who made a very good queen consort, and who did nothing to deserve her fate at the hands of the executioner on 19th May 1536, or the blackening of her name.

However, she was not the only victim of those bloody days of 1536.

In May 1536, five men were executed for high treason for having had sexual relationships with Queen Anne Boleyn and for conspiring with her to kill the king. Another two men were imprisoned but later released without charge. Wives lost husbands, children lost fathers, parents lost sons, names were tarnished, goods, offices and lands that provided families with incomes were seized… It is hard to fully understand the impact on the families of those linked to the fall of Anne Boleyn in 1536.

So, who were the men who were caught up in Anne's fall?

George Boleyn

The most important man executed in May 1536, as far as status is concerned, was George Boleyn, Lord Rochford. He was, of course, Anne's brother. I find him a fascinating figure, and Clare Cherry and I obviously wrote a book on him, but in this article, I'll just give you a potted history of his life.

George was the only surviving son of Thomas Boleyn and his wife, Elizabeth Howard. We don't know the birthdates of the Boleyn children, but it is likely that he was born circa 1504/5. He was probably born at Blickling Hall as his father didn't move the family down to Hever until 1505/6, but it is possible that George was born at Hever. It's certainly the only home he'd remember. Very little is known of George's early life and education, but his fluency in French led his 19th-century biographer, Edmond Bapst to speculate that he may have travelled on diplomatic missions with his father as he was growing up, or perhaps he spent some time there in his youth, being educated.

The sons of wealthy families were educated at home by private tutors until attending university from around the age of 14. George's language skills (he knew French, Latin and some Italian) are evidence of an excellent education, as are his keen interest in theology and literature, and his gifts of poetry and translation. Although there is no surviving record of him attending Oxford University, he was said by Anthony Wood, in the 17th century, to have been educated amongst the Oxonians.

George took part in the Christmas festivities of 1514/15, playing a part in the mummery, and he was appointed as one of Henry VIII's pages in around 1516. He lost this position in 1526, as part of Cardinal Wolsey's Eltham Ordinances, which were designed to remove those who were young and popular with the king, from the privy chamber, but he was compensated with the post of cupbearer to the king instead, meaning that he would have been present to serve the king at every state occasion. In 1528, he was made an esquire of the body and in the mid to late

1520s he was rewarded for his service and for his closeness to the king with grants, including the manor of Grimston in Norfolk which seems to have been a wedding present from the king for George's marriage to Jane Parker, daughter of Lord Morley.

George was knighted in 1529, and at the end of the year, he took his father's title of Viscount Rochford when his father was elevated to the earldom of Wiltshire. He was also made a gentleman of the privy chamber that year. In 1530 he joined the privy council.

Thomas Boleyn, with his gift for languages and his way with people, was one of Henry VIII's trusted diplomats and it appears that he expected George to follow in his footsteps and become a diplomat for the king. In October 1529, at the age of just 24 or 25, George was sent on his first diplomatic mission to France, one that would last four months, and this would be followed soon after by another six diplomatic visits. The principal object of George's first foreign embassy was to persuade the universities of France to find in favour of Henry's divorce from Catherine. It was on this visit and the ones shortly after that George developed good relations with King Francis I and his sister Marguerite of Angouleme. This relationship was something that would help on future missions, such as the one in 1533 when George was tasked with telling Francis I that Henry VIII had married Anne Boleyn and to persuade him to join with others in urging the pope to accept the marriage.

Foreign diplomacy wasn't the only thing with which King Henry VIII trusted George Boleyn. In 1531, George was chosen by Henry VIII to express his growing anti-papal sentiments and Parliament's arguments in favour of supremacy to Convocation. A twenty-six-year-old man appearing before convocation must have been quite a spectacle. George was also active in the Reformation Parliament, the parliament which sat from October 1529-1536 and which passed the main pieces of legislation which led to the English Reformation. He wasn't officially called to the Parliament until Feb 1533, but he maintained a prominent role until his fall. In 1534, the key year seeing as it was the year that the Acts of Succession and Supremacy were passed, the average attendance of the Lords Temporal for Parliament was just 22 out of 46, George's attendance was 41 times even though he was away for two months on a diplomatic mission. He was committed to his job.

In 1534, George was made Lord Warden of the Cinque Ports and Constable of Dover Castle. The position of Lord Warden was a powerful appointment and showed just how high George was in the king's favour. It was a surprising appointment for a man who was just 29/30.

George was also a gifted poet. Although nothing survives today which is attributed to him, he was considered by his contemporaries to be as talented as Thomas Wyatt the Elder and Henry Howard, Earl of Surrey. Court chronicler Raphael Holinshed writes that "He wrote divers songs and sonnets", Anthony Wood in the 17th century explained that at Oxford "his natural inclinations to poetry were discovered and admired by his contemporaries", and George Cavendish, gentleman usher to Cardinal Wolsey, praised him by saying "Dame eloquence also taught me the art, In meter and verse to make pleasant ditties." Sixteenth-century dramatist and historian John Bale wrote of his "rhythmos elegantissimos". A passage of verse, written by Richard Smith in 1575 and prefixed to a selection of poems written by George Gascoigne, confirms George's verse skills by including him amongst such worthies as Chaucer, Surrey and Wyatt:

> "Chaucer by writing purchast fame,
> And Gower got a worthy name:
> Sweet Surrey suckt Parnassus springs,
> And Wiat wrote of wondrous things:
> Olde Rochford clambe the statelie throne
> Which Muses hold in Helicone
> Then thither let good Gascoigne go,
> For sure his verse deserveth so."

Surrey was executed as a traitor, and we still have poetry from him, so there must have been a concerted effort to get rid of things related to the Boleyn siblings.

However, 16th-century historian John Bale, who made use of 16th-century author Sir John Harington's manuscripts, attributed a poem called "The Lover Complaineth the Unkindness of his Love" to George Boleyn. Tottell's Miscellany attributed the poem to Sir Thomas Wyatt the Elder, but as Clare Cherry and I point out in our book on George, Sir John Harington was meticulous in his attribution of poems, all the others in his MS are correctly attributed, so there's a good chance that it was written by George Boleyn. Horace Walpole, 3rd Earl of Orford, went with Harington's attribution in his 1806 "Catalogue of Royal and Noble Authors of England, Scotland and Ireland.

> MY lute, awake, perform the last
> Labour, that thou and I shall waste;
> And end that I have now begun:
> And when this song is sung and past,
> My lute, be still, for I have done.
>
> As to be heard where ear is none;
> As lead to grave in marble stone;
> My song may pierce her heart as soon.
> Should we then sigh, or sing, or moan?
> No, no, my lute, for I have done.
>
> The rocks do not so cruelly
> Repulse the waves continually,
> As she my suit and affection:
> So that I am past remedy;
> Whereby my lute and I have done.
>
> Proud of the spoil that thou hast got
> Of simple hearts through Love's shot,

By whom unkind thou hast them won:
Think not he hath his bow forgot,
Although my lute and I have done.

Vengeance shall fall on thy disdain,
That makest but game on earnest pain;
Think not alone under the sun
Unquit to cause thy lovers plain;
Although my lute and I have done.

May chance thee lie withered and old
In winter nights, that are so cold,
Plaining in vain unto the moon;
Thy wishes then dare not be told:
Care then who list, for I have done.

And then may chance thee to repent
The time that thou hast lost and spent,
To cause thy lovers sigh and swoon:
Then shalt thou know beauty but lent,
And wish and want as I have done.

Now cease, my lute, this is the last
Labour, that thou and I shall waste;
And ended is that we begun:
Now is this song both sung and past;
My lute, be still, for I have done.

George wasn't only one of the king's diplomats, he was the
king's friend. We know from the king's accounts, regarding
payments made to George, that they played shovelboard, bowls,
tennis, primero (a popular card game) and also enjoyed hunting
and archery together. The king liked to surround himself with
young men who enjoyed such sports, as well as jousting, which
George also enjoyed, and men who were entertaining and

intelligent. George fit the bill.

How did this young man's world come crashing down?

It's impossible to date the beginning of the end for the Boleyns. In the summer of 1534, George was riding high, and his sister, the queen, was pregnant. However, Anne either lost that baby to a premature stillbirth, or it was a phantom pregnancy. I wonder if it was at this point that the king started to worry that history was repeating itself. Anne was certainly worried about her marriage for she plotted with her sister-in-law, Jane Boleyn, that autumn to remove a woman from court who had caught the king's fancy. It was also that autumn that the English court received a visit from the Admiral of France, a visit that didn't go according to plan and showed that an alliance with France against the Empire could not be relied upon.

France was still not playing ball in 1535, and it became increasingly clear that England needed to reconcile with Spain, but then Queen Anne was an obstacle to that. In January 1536, Catherine of Aragon died, Anne Boleyn miscarried a male foetus, and Henry VIII was reminded of his mortality when he suffered a jousting accident. Henry was also flirting with one of his wife's ladies: Jane Seymour. With Catherine gone, Henry could get rid of Anne without being forced to go back to his first wife, AND with Anne out of the way, he could ally England with Spain and have a new wife who could give him a son.

Now, I believe that Henry VIII was behind Anne's fall. I believe that he had become convinced that his marriage to Anne was as cursed as his marriage to Catherine, and that Anne had become an obstacle to foreign policy. I think he tasked Cromwell with getting rid of her and getting rid of her in a very final manner. He'd left Catherine alive, and she'd been a thorn in his side for years, Anne had to go properly. Cromwell set about plotting, and for him, a plot against the queen was also a way for him to get rid of men who he saw as a bad influence on the king. Just like Cardinal Wolsey had used the Eltham Ordinances to get rid of privy chamberers who he saw as being too young and influential, Cromwell could use legal action against Anne to have a bit of a clear-out. He was a legal whiz, and I'm sure that left to his own devices he could have come up with a much more watertight case than he did, but I think Henry VIII couldn't stop himself meddling. The Boleyns had to be brought down. He'd heard that George and Anne had ridiculed his clothes, his poetry, and Anne had spoken of his sexual prowess or rather lack of it. He needed revenge, and he needed to completely blacken their names, hence the outrageous incest charge.

But how did the other men become involved in this plot against the queen?

Let me tell you a little about them…

Mark Smeaton

The fact that Mark Smeaton was known as "Mark" at court, a familiar address, points to him being of lowly origins and also probably younger than his contemporaries at court. It is thought that his family were Flemish and that his father was a carpenter, but we don't know much else about his background.

He had a talent for singing and for playing instruments like the portable organ, lute and virginals, and he was talent-spotted by Cardinal Wolsey for his choir. After Wolsey's fall, Smeaton joined the choir of the Chapel Royal, and in 1529 he joined Henry VIII's privy chamber. As I explain in my book on Anne's fall, the Privy Purse Expenses of November 1529 to December 1532 show frequent mentions of "marke". In the introduction, the editor of the expenses explains that it is clear that Smeaton was "wholly supported and clothed" by Henry VIII. There are many mentions of payments for "shert"s and "hosen". His rise in favour is evident from the increase in his rewards during the period, from "xx s" (20 shillings) in December 1530 to "iii li. vi s. viii d." (£3 6 shillings and 8 pence) in October 1532.

We know that he was part of a circle that included George Boleyn and Thomas Wyatt because his name is inscribed on a book which belonged to George and which was also inscribed by Wyatt. This book was a copy of Jean Lefèvre's translation of Mathieu of Boulogne's 13th-century satirical poem "Liber lamentationum Matheoluli", a text that was widely circulated by scholars at the time. These friends were obviously enjoying passing around a trendy book, much like friends do today.

On 29th April 1536, Queen Anne Boleyn encountered Mark standing in the round window of her presence chamber. She asked him why he was looking so sad and, according to Anne, he replied that "it was no matter". Anne goes on to describe what happened next:

> "And then I said, You may not look to have me speak to you as I should do to a noble man, because ye be an inferior person. No, no, said he, a look sufficeth me; and thus fare you well."

It sounds like Anne was irritated by his sulky behaviour and his answer, which I guess would be like someone giving a shoulder shrug today. It was not the answer expected by a queen from a lowly court musician. John Strype, the 18th-century historian, wondered if it was Anne's reaction to him which made Smeaton want to "take this opportunity to humble her; and revenge himself".

Mark was apprehended the next day and taken to Thomas Cromwell's house in Stepney, where, after being interrogated for 24 hours, he was said to have confessed to sleeping with the queen on three occasions.

Sir Henry Norris

Sir Henry Norris was born sometimes in the late 1490s and was the son of Richard Norris. His paternal grandparents were Sir William Norris of Yattendon and Jane de Vere, daughter of John de Vere, twelfth Earl of Oxford. Norris's family had a long history of serving the monarch – his great-grandfather, Sir John Norris, had been Keeper of the Great Wardrobe to Henry VI and his grandfather, Sir William Norris, had been Knight of the Body to Edward IV.

Sometime before 1526, Sir Henry Norris married Mary Fiennes, daughter of Thomas Fiennes, eighth Baron Dacre. The couple had three children. Norris was left a widower in around 1530.

He received his first royal grant in 1515, and by 1517 he had joined Henry VIII's privy chamber. In 1518, he was made a gentleman of the privy chamber and was handling money for the king. In 1519, he was rewarded with an annuity of 50 marks – evidence of the king's favour. He attended the king at the Field of the Cloth of Gold in 1520

He survived Wolsey's purge of the privy chamber, and he took over the position of Groom of the Stool and Keeper of the Privy Purse, posts that were surrendered by William Compton. Although helping the king use the closed stool, i.e. helping the king go to the toilet, and also monitoring the king's bowel movements and digestive health, sounds like an awful job to us today, it was the highest position in the privy chamber. It was a position of responsibility and trust, and also influence. The groom of the stool had the king's ear, and a few years later the role became incorporated with Chief Gentleman of the Privy Chamber, so Norris was in charge of the privy chamber.

His role was one of intimacy, and people recognised his influence and would petition him to speak to the king on their behalf. You didn't want to fall out with the groom of the stool, and then him speak against you in his private moments with the king. He also controlled access to the king's private chamber and to the king himself. He was a useful patron to have.

Eric Ives writes that "for the rest of his life he remained the king's most intimate servant and confidant". He accompanied Henry VIII and Anne Boleyn to inspect York Place, which they renamed Whitehall, after Cardinal Wolsey surrendered it to the king, and he went with them to Calais in 1532. It is also believed that he attended their wedding on 25th January 1533. He received many royal grants and offices for his loyal service to the king and as a valued and respected friend. Offices included: Chamberlain of North Wales, Black Rod, Master of the Hart Hounds and of the Hawks, Graver of the Tower of London, High Steward of the University of Oxford etc. His revenue added up to make him wealthier than many of the leading nobles at that time.

So what happened?

Well, Eric Ives writes that "as Thomas Cromwell rose in royal service, the groom stood in the way of his wish to control the patronage machine." There's no evidence of any friction or enmity between the two men, but as well as acting as a patron, Norris, as head of the privy chamber, was also a leader of like-minded men. He'd become very influential, rich and powerful, and was also helping others rise, others that might not suit Cromwell.

Norris was close to both the king and queen. He shared the queen's evangelical views, and his son had been tutored along with her ward Henry Carey by Nicholas Bourbon, a man Anne had helped escape from prison in France. He was also courting Anne's cousin and lady, Margaret Shelton. Like any Renaissance queen, Anne enjoyed the tradition of courtly love, and male courtiers would flirt, in a chivalric sense with their queen. Unfortunately, on the last weekend in April 1536, Anne and Norris had an altercation which took the tradition a bit too far. Instead of Norris initiating the flirtation, Anne acted as the aggressor and asked Norris why he was taking so much time in marrying her cousin. When he gave her a non-committal answer, she said "You look for dead men's shoes, for if aught came to the King but good, you would look to have me", thus accusing Norris of delaying his marriage to Margaret because he fancied her. A horrified Norris replied that "if he [should have any such thought] he would his head were off." Norris was horrified because Anne had mentioned the king's death.

Although the date of this conversation was not listed on the later indictments, Norris was one of the men charged with sleeping with the king and conspiring with her to kill the king. On 1st May 1536, at the annual May Day joust at Greenwich, Norris led the defenders while George Boleyn led the challengers. Norris was armed and ready to joust when his horse refused to run. The King stepped in and offered Norris his own horse – an act of kindness and chivalry. However, later in the day, the king suddenly abandoned the joust and ordered Norris to return with him to Westminster. George Constantine, one of Norris's servants, recorded that the king interrogated Norris on their journey and promised him a pardon if he would confess. Norris would not confess, and the next day he was taken to the Tower. Gilbert Burnet, Bishop of Salisbury, writing in the 17th century, wrote that Norris said "that in his conscience he thought her innocent of these things laid to her charge; but whether she was or not, he would not accuse her of anything; and he would die a thousand times, rather than ruin an innocent person."

Sir Francis Weston

Sir Francis Weston was born about 1511 to Richard Weston, a former Under-Treasurer of the Exchequer, and his wife, Anne Sandys who had been one of Catherine of Aragon' s ladies. Francis married Anne Pickering in May 1530, and they had a son, Henry, in 1535.

By 1526, he was at the royal court serving as a page. In 1532, Weston became a gentleman of the privy chamber, and in 1533 he was made joint governor of Guernsey with his father. He was also made a Knight of the Bath in 1533 as part of the celebrations for Anne Boleyn's coronation. The grants, pensions and other rewards that the king gave him are evidence that he was a royal favourite. We know from the king's expenses that, like George Boleyn, he would often play tennis, bowls and card games with the king, for example, in 1530, the king paid him, 16 angels, after Weston beat him at tennis four times.

Although he was married, it appears that he had taken an interest in Margaret Shelton, one of the queen's ladies and the same one that was being courted by Sir Henry Norris. During her time in the Tower of London in May 1536, Anne Boleyn remembered that she had accosted Weston because he loved Madge and not his wife and he replied that he "loved one in her house better than them both". She asked who, and he replied "it is yourself", at which Anne said she defied him, i.e. she rebuked him. Unfortunately, Anne's words regarding her conversation with Weston were recorded and passed on to Sir William Kingston, Constable of the Tower of London, who, in turn, passed them on to Thomas Cromwell. Weston was arrested on 4th May 1536 and taken to the Tower of London.

Weston's parents and wife made strenuous attempts to save Francis in 1536, offering the king money in return for his life, as did the French ambassadors, Antoine de Castelnau (Bishop of Tarbes) and Jean, Sieur de Dinteville, but nothing could save him.

William Brereton

William Brereton was the sixth son of a leading landowning Cheshire family. He was born 1487-90 and was the son of Sir Randolph Brereton of Malpas, chamberlain of the county palatine of Cheshire. Like three of his brothers before him, he entered royal service, and by 1524 he was serving Henry VIII as a groom of the privy chamber. He married Lady Elizabeth Savage, widow of Sir John Savage of Clifton, Cheshire, and daughter of Charles Somerset, 1st Earl of Worcester, the King's second cousin, in around 1529/30.

Eric Ives writes of how Brereton was "the dominant royal servant in Cheshire and north Wales" due to his wealth, his royal grants and his father's power in Cheshire, and he became chamberlain of Chester in 1530 following the death of his father. By that time, he already held a host of offices and positions in the region.

In 1530, he and Thomas Wriothesley rode around England collecting signatures for the petition to be presented to the pope in support of the king's quest for an annulment of his first marriage. In 1531, the king chose him to deliver jewels to Anne Boleyn, and like Norris, he may have been present at the king's secret marriage to Anne in January 1533. Following the annulment of Henry VIII's marriage to Catherine of Aragon, he was made receiver-general in Cheshire and Flint to Catherine, in her new position as Dowager Princess of Wales. He was listed as one of those who attended Anne's coronation celebrations when Henry VIII dubbed around 50 knights bachelor. He also accompanied Henry and Anne on many hunting trips.

He seems to have had a dark side. He appears to have used his position, like many in those times, for his own gain. John ap Griffith Eyton, his former duty, accused Brereton of various offences including the robbery of cattle and even the murders of three people. Brereton denied the charges and accused Eyton of one of the murders instead. Eyton was acquitted by a court in London but then rearrested, imprisoned and eventually hanged. This was down to Brereton, apparently.

Like Norris, Brereton was a powerful and influential man. Cromwell had plans for administrative reform in North Wales, and Brereton opposed them. With his colourful reputation, he was perhaps an easy target for Cromwell and Anne's fall was the perfect opportunity to get rid of this thorn in his side. However, even though Cardinal Wolsey's servant George Cavendish wrote of Brereton's persecution of the innocent and bad ways, he concluded by saying "yf any of them was innocent, it was he".

Thomas Wyatt the Elder

Poet and diplomat Sir Thomas Wyatt the Elder was one of two men imprisoned in the Tower of London in May 1536 but released later that summer without charge.

Wyatt was born in 1503 at Allington Castle in Kent, not far from the Boleyn family home of Hever Castle. His father, Sir Henry Wyatt had been imprisoned in Richard III's reign as a Lancastrian supporter and subsequently released on Henry VII's accession. Henry Wyatt had been a privy councillor for Henry VII and was an executor of his will; he carried on in service to the new king, Henry VIII.

Thomas served as a sewer extraordinary at Princess Mary's christening in 1516 and was educated at the humanist St John's College, Cambridge. He married Elizabeth Brooke, the daughter of Lord Cobham, in 1520 and in 1521 Elizabeth gave birth to their son, Thomas, who would, of course, grow up to be the Thomas Wyatt who led Wyatt's Rebellion in Mary I's reign.

Wyatt started his court career properly in 1524 at the age of 21 when he became clerk of the king's jewels. He was made Esquire of the Body in 1525 and then went on to become a diplomat for the king, undertaking many foreign missions including one to France in 1526 and one to the Papal Court in Rome in 1527. He was made High Marshal of Calais in 1528, and in 1532 he was made Commissioner of the Peace in Essex. Wyatt was also one of the men chosen to accompany the King and Anne Boleyn on their visit to Calais in late 1532, and he served Anne at her coronation in the summer of 1533. He was knighted in 1535.

His marriage to Elizabeth Brooke was an unhappy one, and the couple appears to have been estranged by the mid-1520s. It is around then that he appears to have been linked romantically to Anne Boleyn, who returned to England from France in late 1521. Wyatt had little to offer Anne, with being married, but it appears that he was infatuated with her and that she was his muse.

According to one story related by George Wyatt, his grandson, Thomas Wyatt playfully snatched a jewel from Anne and kept it as a trophy. One day, he was playing bowls with Henry VIII, who was courting Anne, and the men argued over a shot. The king pointed to the wood with the finger on which he was wearing Anne's ring and declared "Wyatt, I tell thee it is mine". Wyatt, seeing the trophy on the king's finger, replied "If it may like your majesty to give me leave to measure it, I

hope it will be mine", and he took Anne's jewel from around his
neck and began to measure the cast with its ribbon. A furious
Henry VIII broke up the game and went in search of Anne for
an explanation.

There is no evidence that Wyatt's love for Anne was requited.
His poem *Whoso List to Hunt* tells of a man hunting a hind
(Anne), with little chance of success, and then being forced to
withdraw from the hunt because of another hunter (Henry VIII).

> "[…]Who list her hunt, I put him out of doubt,
> As well as I may spend his time in vain.
> And graven with diamonds in letters plain
> There is written, her fair neck round about:
> *Noli me tangere*, for Caesar's I am,
> And wild for to hold, though I seem tame."

It must be this previous link to Anne and his friendship with
George that led to him being arrested in 1536. It was probably
his father's good relationship with Cromwell that saved Wyatt.

Wyatt carried on in service to the king. He was made steward
of Conisburgh Castle during the Pilgrimage of Grace rebellion
and was asked to provide 200 men for the king's side. He also
served as sheriff of Kent and in 1537 carried out a diplomatic
mission to Charles V's court, an unsuccessful one. Wyatt got
into trouble again in 1541 when he was charged with treason
for making rude comments about the King and dealing with
Cardinal Pole. Wyatt was once again imprisoned in the Tower of
London, and this time he had no father to secure his release, his
father had died in November 1536. This time, it was Catherine
Howard, Henry VIII's fifth wife, who secured his pardon and
release, but Wyatt had to agree to return to his estranged wife. In
1542, Wyatt was back in favour and had been restored to his
office of ambassador. However, his return to favour was shortlived
because Wyatt was taken ill after receiving the emperor's envoy at
Falmouth. Sir Thomas Wyatt died on the 11th October 1542 at
Clifton Maybank House, the home of his friend Sir John Horsey,

in Sherborne Dorset.

Sir Richard Page

Like Wyatt, Sir Richard Page was imprisoned in the Tower in May 1536 but then released without charge.

Nothing is known about his background and early life, all we know is that he started his career in service to Cardinal Wolsey as his chamberlain and in 1516 he was listed as a gentleman of the privy chamber and was referred to as "Sir" Richard Page.

In the 1520s, he served as a Justice for the Peace for Surrey and Middlesex, and in 1525 he was chosen to help administer the household of Henry VIII's illegitimate son, Henry Fitzroy, Duke of Richmond and Somerset. In 1527, he accompanied Wolsey to Calais, and in 1528 he was a surveyor and receiver for the ports of London and Southampton with Sir John Wallop. He profited from the fall of his former master, Wolsey in 1530, being granted manors and lands. He was married to Elizabeth Stanhope (nee Bourchier), widow of Sir Edward Stanhope and mother of Anne Stanhope, the future Duchess of Somerset. He was her fourth husband. They had a daughter Elizabeth.

He was a close friend of Queen Anne, carrying out sundry little services for her and being rewarded for doing so, and this combined with his rivalry with Sir Nicholas Carew, a Seymour supporter, in the privy chamber may have been responsible for his arrest in 1536. However, his good relationship with men like Sir John Russell and Sir William Fitzwilliam probably saved him from an untimely death. It did put him off serving the king though. He wrote to Lady Lisle "he has not greatly assayed to be a daily courtier again". However, he did pick himself up and carried on in service to the king, accompanying the king on a journey to do with the Pilgrimage of Grace, serving as a sheriff, as Lieutenant of the gentleman pensioners, chamberlain to Prince Edward's household at Hampton Court. He died in 1548

Their Ends

George Boleyn, Lord Rochford, Sir Henry Norris, Sir Francis
Weston, William Brereton and Mark Smeaton were executed on
17th May 1536. They had all been found guilty of high treason –
Norris, Weston, Brereton and Smeaton at a special commission
of oyer and terminer on 12th May 1536 at Westminster Hall,
and Rochford by a jury of his peers in the Great Hall of the
Tower of London on 15th May. They all pleaded innocent apart
from Mark, who pleaded guilty. They were sentenced to death,
a full traitor's death, but their sentences were later commuted to
beheading. They were escorted to the scaffold on Tower Hill and
beheaded in order of rank: Rochford, Norris, Weston, Brereton
and Smeaton.

Rochford made quite a speech, using this last opportunity to
talk of his reformed faith:

"Christian men, I am born under the law, and judged
under the law, and die under the law, and the law has
condemned me. Masters all, I am not come hither for to
preach, but for to die, for I have deserved for to die if I had
20 lives, more shamefully than can be devised, for I am a
wretched sinner, and I have sinned shamefully, I have knowne
no man so evil, and to rehearse my sins openly it were no
pleasure to you to hear them, nor yet for me to rehearse them,
for God knoweth all.

Therefore, masters all, I pray you take heed by me, and
especially my lords and gentlemen of the court, the which I
have been among, take heed by me, and beware of such a
fall, and I pray to God the Father, the Son, and the Holy
Ghost, three persons and one God, that my death may be an
example unto you all, and beware, trust not in the vanity of
the world, and especially in the flattering of the court. And I
cry God mercy, and ask all the world forgiveness, as willingly
as I would have forgiveness of God; and if I have offended any
man that is not here now, either in thought, word, or deed,

and if you hear any such, I pray you heartily on my behalf, pray them to forgive me for God's sake. And yet, my masters all, I have one thing for to say to you, men do come and say that I have been a setter forth of the word of God, and one that have favoured the Gospel of Christ; and because I would not that God's word should be slandered by me, I say unto you all, that if I had followed God's word in deed as I did read it and set it forth to my power, I had not come to this. I did read the Gospel of Christ, but I did not follow it; if I had, I had been a live man among you: therefore I pray you, masters all, for God's sake stick to the truth and follow it, for one good follower is worth three readers, as God knoweth."

Norris was recorded as saying almost nothing at all, Weston addressed the crowd, saying, "I had thought to have lived in abomination yet this twenty or thirty years and then to have made amends. I thought little it would have come to this. Brereton repeated the phrase "I have deserved to dye if it were a thousande deethes. But the cause wherfore I dye, judge not. But yf ye judge, judge the best." And Smeaton said, "Masters I pray you all praye for me, for I have deserved the deeth".

When Anne Boleyn heard that Mark had gone to his death without retracting his confession, she cried: "Did he not exonerate me [...] before he died, of the public infamy he laid on me? Alas! I fear his soul will suffer for it."

There is no mention of Mark showing any sign of being tortured when he went to the scaffold on the day, but physical torture is not the only way to get a false confession. A full traitor's death involved the alleged criminal being drawn to the place of execution attached to a wooden hurdle and drawn by a horse, being hanged until he was nearly dead, having his genitals cut off and burnt in front of him, being disembowelled and his organs burnt, and then being beheaded and quartered. It was the executioner's job to keep the person alive for as long as possible for the bloodthirsty spectators. I can imagine giving a false confession in return for a merciful death if I was told I was going to die anyway.

Norris, Weston, Brereton and Smeaton were buried in the churchyard of St Peter ad Vincula, and Rochford was buried in the chapel's chancel.

Wyatt's Poetry

Wyatt was still imprisoned in the Tower when Anne and the men were executed on 17th May and 19th May 1536, and he wrote poetry to convey his feelings regarding the deaths of his friends and colleagues.

This one is about each of the men:

> "In mourning wise since daily I increase,
> Thus should I cloak the cause of all my grief;
> So pensive mind with tongue to hold his peace'
> My reason sayeth there can be no relief:
> Wherefore give ear, I humbly you require,
> The affect to know that thus doth make me moan.
> The cause is great of all my doleful cheer
> For those that were, and now be dead and gone.
> What thought to death desert be now their call.
> As by their faults it doth appear right plain?
> Of force I must lament that such a fall should light on
> those so
> wealthily did reign,
> Though some perchance will say, of cruel heart,
> A traitor's death why should we thus bemoan?
> But I alas, set this offence apart,
> Must needs bewail the death of some be gone.
>
> As for them all I do not thus lament,
> But as of right my reason doth me bind;
> But as the most doth all their deaths repent,
> Even so do I by force of mourning mind.

Some say, 'Rochford, haddest thou been not so proud,
For thy great wit each man would thee bemoan,
Since as it is so, many cry aloud
It is great loss that thou art dead and gone.'

Ah! Norris, Norris, my tears begin to run
To think what hap did thee so lead or guide
Whereby thou hast both thee and thine undone
That is bewailed in court of every side;
In place also where thou hast never been
Both man and child doth piteously thee moan.
They say, 'Alas, thou art far overseen
By thine offences to be thus dead and gone.'

Ah! Weston, Weston, that pleasant was and young,
In active things who might with thee compare?
All words accept that thou diddest speak with tongue,
So well esteemed with each where thou diddest fare.
And we that now in court doth lead our life
Most part in mind doth thee lament and moan;
But that thy faults we daily hear so rife,
All we should weep that thou are dead and gone.

Brereton farewell, as one that least I knew.
Great was thy love with divers as I hear,
But common voice doth not so sore thee rue
As other twain that doth before appear;
But yet no doubt but they friends thee lament
And other hear their piteous cry and moan.
So doth each heart for thee likewise relent
That thou givest cause thus to be dead and gone.

Ah! Mark, what moan should I for thee make more,
Since that thy death thou hast deserved best,
Save only that mine eye is forced sore

With piteous plaint to moan thee with the rest?
A time thou haddest above thy poor degree,
The fall whereof thy friends may well bemoan:
A rotten twig upon so high a tree
Hath slipped thy hold, and thou art dead and gone.

And thus farewell each one in hearty wise!
The axe is home, your heads be in the street;
The trickling tears doth fall so from my eyes
I scarce may write, my paper is so wet.
But what can hope when death hath played his part,
Though nature's course will thus lament and moan?
Leave sobs therefore, and every Christian heart
Pray for the souls of those be dead and gone."

I find it interesting that he calls Mark "a rotten twig upon so high a tree". He is sympathetic about the others but not so about Mark, this must surely be because of Mark's confession.

And Wyatt's other poem:

"Who list his wealth and ease retain,
Himself let him unknown contain.
Press not too fast in at that gate
Where the return stands by disdain,
For sure, circa Regna tonat.

The high mountains are blasted oft
When the low valley is mild and soft.
Fortune with Health stands at debate.
The fall is grievous from aloft.
And sure, circa Regna tonat.

These bloody days have broken my heart.
My lust, my youth did them depart,
And blind desire of estate.

Who hastes to climb seeks to revert.
Of truth, circa Regna tonat.

The Bell Tower showed me such sight
That in my head sticks day and night.
There did I learn out of a grate,
For all favour, glory, or might,
That yet circa Regna tonat.

By proof, I say, there did I learn:
Wit helpeth not defence too yerne,
Of innocency to plead or prate.
Bear low, therefore, give God the stern,
For sure, circa Regna tonat."

Note that Wyatt writes here that a defence of innocence doesn't help; neither does the use of wit. It is clear that he views his friends and former love as innocent and knows that nothing can help someone who is close to the throne and who then falls.

"The Bell Tower showed me such sight
That in my head sticks day and night."

Wyatt was obviously traumatised by what happened, and I expect it was something that stuck with him for the rest of his life – he died just six years later. Like the men's families, he was expected to put it all behind him and carry on in loyal service to the king. That was their duty. Modern people criticise them for that. We ask "how could they go back to court and serve the king?" but don't forget that these families had mouths to feed, that they had to think about those that were left, their futures, and that also the king was God's anointed sovereign. God had chosen him as the country's leader, and it was their duty to serve him loyally. These people had their reputation to rebuild.

But, I'm sure that they would never forget that "for sure, circa Regna tonat" - around the throne the thunder rolls. Service and wealth could come at a great cost.

Notes and Sources

Ives, Eric (2004) *The Life and Death of Anne Boleyn*, Wiley-Blackwell.

Cherry, Claire, and Ridgway, Claire (2014) *George Boleyn: Tudor Poet, Courtier and Diplomat*, MadeGlobal Publishing.

Bapst, Edmond (translated by MacFarlane, J.A, edited by Ridgway, Claire, 2013) *Two Gentleman Poets at the Court of Henry VIII: George Boleyn and Henry Howard*, MadeGlobal Publishing.

ed. Nicolas, Nicholas Harris (1827) *The privy purse expenses of King Henry the Eighth, from November 1529, to December 1532: with introductory remarks and illustrative notes*, William Pickering.

Burrow, C. (2015, May 28). Wyatt, Sir Thomas (c. 1503–1542), poet and ambassador. Oxford Dictionary of National Biography.

Brigden, Susan (2014) *Thomas Wyatt: The Heart's Forest*, Faber & Faber.

Shulman, Nicola (2013) *Graven with Diamonds: The Many Lives of Thomas Wyatt: Poet, Lover, Statesman, and Spy in the Court of Henry VIII*, Steerforth Press.

Ives, E. (2008, January 03). Brereton, William (c. 1487x90–1536), courtier and administrator. Oxford Dictionary of National Biography.

Ives, E. (2009, May 21). Norris, Henry (b. before 1500, d. 1536), courtier. Oxford Dictionary of National Biography.

Hughes, J. (2004, September 23). Weston, Sir Francis (1511–1536), courtier. Oxford Dictionary of National Biography.

Davies, C. (2008, January 03). Page, Sir Richard (d. 1548), courtier. Oxford Dictionary of National Biography.

Cavendish, George (1827 edition) *The Life of Cardinal Wolsey*, Printed for Harding and Lepard.

"A Memorial from George Constantyne to Thomas, Lord Cromwell", Archaeologia, or, Miscellaneous Tracts Relating to Antiquity, 23 (1831).

Letters and Papers, Foreign and Domestic, Henry VIII, Volume 10, January-June 1536, ed. James Gairdner (London, 1887), British History Online http://www.british-history.ac.uk/letters-papers-hen8/vol10.

Calendar of State Papers, Spain, Volume 5 Part 2, 1536-1538, ed. Pascual de Gayangos (London, 1888), British History Online http://www.british-history.ac.uk/cal-state-papers/spain/vol5/no2.

Hall, Edward (1809) *Hall's chronicle: containing the history of England, during the reign of Henry the Fourth, and the succeeding monarchs, to the end of the reign of Henry the Eighth, in which are particularly described the manners and customs of those periods*, J. Johnson.

Wriothesley, Charles (1875) *A chronicle of England during the reigns of the Tudors, from A.D. 1485 to 1559*, Volume I, Camden Society.

19 May 1536 – To Jesus Christ I commend my soul

I'm not sure whether Anne Boleyn got any sleep on the night of the 18th May. She was certainly up at dawn, celebrating the Mass and receiving the sacrament from her almoner John Skip. She then ate breakfast and waited for Sir William Kingston, Constable of the Tower of London, to come and collect her.

At 8 am, Kingston informed the waiting queen that the time of her death was near and that she should get herself ready. But Anne was ready. She had taken special care with her outfit – the ermine trim symbolised royalty and crimson, the colour of her kirtle, was associated with martyrdom. Her hood was the traditional English gable hood, rather than her usual stylish French hood.

Sir William Kingston escorted the queen from her apartments in the royal palace past the Great Hall, through Cole Harbour Gate (Cold Harbour Gate), and along the western side of the White Tower to the black-draped scaffold. The site of the scaffold built for Anne Boleyn was not where the glass memorial stands today on Tower Green but "before the house of Ordnance", i.e. on the parade ground between the White Tower and the present day entrance to the Crown Jewels. Anne climbed the scaffold steps with Kingston's assistance and then addressed the waiting crowd:

> "Good Christian people, I have not come here to preach a sermon; I have come here to die. For according to the law and by the law I am judged to die, and therefore I will speak nothing against it. I am come hither to accuse no man, nor to speak of that whereof I am accused and condemned to die, but I pray God save the King and send him long to reign over you, for a gentler nor a more merciful prince was there never, and to me he was ever a good, a gentle, and sovereign lord. And if any person will meddle of my cause, I require them to judge the best. And thus I take my leave of the world and of you all, and I heartily desire you all to pray for me."

That speech is corroborated by Edward Hall, George Wyatt, John Foxe and Lord Herbert of Cherbury, but Lancelot de Carles, secretary to the French ambassador, gives a different version in his poem about her death:

> "Oh my friends, friends and more than brothers,
> Since with you I can no longer be,
> And that the course of my years is ended,
> I beg you, not to be unpleasant, /And I
> would like you to pardon me from your good heart
> If I have not used sweetness
> Towards all of you, as I should have,
> Seeing the power and means that I had:
> And I pray you all that by fraternity
> Of Christianity and true charity,
> You give me a place in your devoted prayers
> Toward Jesus, that by the marks
> Of my sins I have not stained
> My soul, after I am gone.
> To tell you why I am here,
> Would not serve you nor me either:

Which is why I am silent, but the judge of the world
In whom justice and truth abound
Knows all, that which of affection
I pray that he will have compassion
For those who judged my death,
And from here when I am dislodged.
You remember that I recommend you to
Your good King in whom I have seen such great
Humanity, and filled with all good things,
Fears God, loves his family,
And great virtue, which I observe
That is happy if God conserves it for you.
Pray then to God that he holds you a long time:
also, that it happens to me
His grace to move me away to him
And to receive my soul today."

People often ask me why Anne Boleyn did not take the opportunity to protest her innocence and why she spoke well of the king. This can be explained. Executions were carefully 'choreographed', with a set format for execution speeches. People were expected to die 'a good death' and accept that they were sinners deserving of death, whether or not they were guilty of the crimes for which they were being executed, and to praise the monarch, who was God's anointed sovereign. People had their surviving loved ones to think about and would not have wanted to tarnish their reputations and standing with the king by dying a dishonourable death. Anne stuck to the usual format for her execution speech. There was no way that she would risk her daughter's safety by defying the king and proclaiming her innocence. Elizabeth's safety and her future relationship with her father must have been paramount in Anne's mind.

After her speech to the crowd, who were "little consoled, [Deeply] desolated to see the poor queen In this state to take in this pain", Anne paid the visibly "distressed" executioner who asked for her forgiveness for what he was about to do. Anne's ladies then removed Anne's mantle, and Anne lifted off her gable hood. "A young lady presented her with a linen cap, with which she covered her hair, and she knelt, fastening her clothes about her feet, and one of the said ladies bandaged her eyes." Anne knelt on the scaffold praying, "O Lord have mercy on me, to God I commend my soul. To Jesus Christ I commend my soul; Lord Jesu receive my soul." As Anne prayed, the executioner called out to his assistant to pass him his sword. As Anne moved her head to try and hear what the assistant was doing, the executioner came up unnoticed behind her and beheaded her with one stroke of his sword.

Anne's ladies, "Who were judged to be nearly dead themselves, From languor and extreme weakness", wrapped her remains in white cloth and took them to the Chapel of St Peter ad Vincula for burial. No casket had been provided, so a yeoman warder fetched an old elm chest which had once contained bow staves from the Tower armoury. Anne's head and body were buried together in the chest in the chancel of the chapel. Cannons fired to let the people of London know that their queen had been executed and Sir Francis Bryan took the news of Anne's death to Jane Seymour.

On that same day, Archbishop Thomas Cranmer issued a dispensation for Henry VIII to marry Jane Seymour "although in the third and third [*Tertio et tertio affinitatis gradibus*] degrees of affinity, without publication of banns."

Notes and Sources

Eric Ives pieced together Anne Boleyn's final walk and the location of the scaffold, which was newly built especially for her, for his book *The Life and Death of Anne Boleyn*, from sources including Anthony Anthony's notes in Lord Herbert's 1679 edition of *The Life and Raigne of Henry VIII*, and *The Lisle Letters* (Volume 3:698), and writes of her being

"beheaded on a new scaffold 'before the house of Ordnance'".
See notes on p.423 of Ives' book.

You can read the original French poem in *Poème sur la Mort
d'Anne Boleyn*, Lancelot de Carles, lines 317-326, in *La
Grande Bretagne devant L'Opinion Française depuis la Guerre
de Cent Ans jusqu'a la Fin du XVI Siècle*, Georges Ascoli. This
translation is from "Anne Boleyn, Lancelot de Carle, and
the Uses of Documentary Evidence", Susan Walters Schmid,
dissertation Arizona State University 2009, pp.170-172.

'Henry VIII: May 1536, 16-20', in Letters and Papers, Foreign
and Domestic, Henry VIII, Volume 10, January-June 1536,
ed. James Gairdner (London, 1887), pp. 371-391. British
History Online http://www.british-history.ac.uk/letters-
papers-hen8/vol10/pp371-391.

Younghusband, George (1919) *The Tower from Within*, Herbert
Jenkins Limited, p.135.

Petition to give Anne Boleyn a royal pardon – Why I'm not signing

In 2015 an e-petition was set up calling on Her Majesty's Government to "Grant Anne Boleyn a royal pardon for the crimes she was wrongly accused of. Let her be reburied in Westminster Abbey with her daughter Elizabeth I. Grant her a royal funeral as she rightly deserved."

This followed on from the campaign by Commander George Melville-Jackson who, in 2005, called on Charles Clarke, the Home Secretary at the time, to pardon Anne Boleyn and to have her remains laid to rest alongside her daughter Elizabeth I. The Wing-Commander worked tirelessly on his campaign, writing to the Queen and historians, consulting a barrister etc. but it was all in vain, and sadly he died without completing his mission.

People kept asking me to share the petition and to spread the word, and although I was happy to mention it, I could not sign it or support it.

How could I, a person who runs an Anne Boleyn site and who spends every day reading and writing about the Boleyns, not support this petition? Didn't I care about Anne? Of course I do, but I have my reasons for not supporting the campaign:

I feel that it's a fruitless endeavour – A barrister told the Wing Commander back in 2005 that it is impossible to go to court and get a judicial review when there is no new evidence. We may believe that Anne was innocent and that it was a tragic miscarriage of justice and we can point out that the dates on the indictments don't make sense, but we cannot prove her innocence after so long. Also, a pardon suggests that she did something for which she needed to be pardoned, and I don't believe that to be true.

What about George Boleyn? Henry Norris? Mark Smeaton? William Brereton? Francis Weston? Margaret Pole? Lady Jane Grey? Archbishop Thomas Cranmer? – I'm sure you can add to that list – Why just Anne? Where do we draw the line?

Westminster Abbey is full – Unless Anne is buried in the same vault as Elizabeth I and Mary I, there just isn't room for her.

Anne is buried as queen – Anne may not have had a fitting burial at the time of her death, but the Victorians who carried out restoration work on the chancel in the Chapel of St Peter ad Vincula buried the remains they thought to be Anne as queen. The remains were "soldered up in thick leaden coffers, and then fastened down with copper screws in boxes made of oak plank, one inch in thickness. Each box bore a leaden escutcheon, on which was engraved the name of the person whose supposed remains were thus enclosed, together with the dates of death, and of the year (1877) of the reinterment." A beautiful memorial tile marks the spot where they buried her remains, and it reads "Queen Anne Boleyn". The chapel is a beautiful place and is a place of worship. I would hate to see the chancel desecrated to exhume Anne when I find it much more peaceful than Westminster Abbey. That tile speaks of Anne's story, and she is remembered with a basket of roses and flowers from visitors every year on 19th May. I don't feel that that could happen at Westminster.

Education is better – For me, it is more important to spend

my time educating people about the story of Anne and the men who fell with her in 1536 rather than campaigning for a pardon for her. I'm not criticising those who feel a pardon is important; it just isn't my priority.

It doesn't change anything – A pardon and moving Anne's remains will not change anything. We cannot rewrite history, and some people will still think she was guilty anyway. Anne is long gone, as is her daughter, and as someone who shares the faith they held I believe that they are in Heaven and have no need for Anne to be pardoned or her remains to be moved.

Fight injustice today instead – Let us campaign for justice for those suffering miscarriages of justice today instead. I know that signing this petition doesn't prevent us from signing others too, and it doesn't mean we don't care about what's happening today, but if we're going to spend a lot of time campaigning for something then let it be something that we can actually change. Support human rights organisations like Amnesty International or take a stand about something that's unfair or abusive in your local community. Anne Boleyn, along with Thomas Cromwell, cared about poor relief, she supported education, she was a charitable woman. While I cannot speak for Anne and say how she'd feel about this petition, I know from her actions in her life that she'd be encouraging of people supporting charities.

There are better things to spend money on – This petition calls for a royal funeral for Anne, something that will cost an awful lot of money. Even if the money was raised through donations, I could still think of better ways to spend that sort of money in Anne's name.

Jane Boleyn, Lady Rochford

This article is based on a talk I did for the Tudor Society back in 2016.

Jane Boleyn, Lady Rochford, was the daughter of Henry Parker, 10th Baron Morley, translator, gentleman usher to Henry VIII and a man who spent his boyhood in the household of Lady Margaret Beaufort, Henry VIII's grandmother. Jane's mother was Alice St John. Jane grew up at the family home in Great Hallingbury, near Bishop's Stortford in Essex

We don't know exactly when Jane came to court, but she was there by 1522 because she played the part of Constancy in the Shrovetide Pageant of the Chateau Vert with other young women like Mary Boleyn, Anne Boleyn and Mary Tudor, Henry VIII's sister. It is thought that Jane married George Boleyn, Anne Boleyn's brother, in late 1524 or early 1525. The couple were childless, or Jane may have suffered from miscarriages or stillbirths, we don't know, but contrary to myth and fiction, there is no evidence that the couple had an unhappy marriage. The couple enjoyed a life of wealth and favour, with George being a favourite of the king and receiving many royal grants.

Unfortunately, when Anne Boleyn was brought down in 1536 on what is thought to be false charges of adultery and conspiring to kill the king, George fell too, being found guilty of committing incest with Anne and plotting with her. Although Jane is often said to have betrayed the Boleyn siblings and to have provided evidence of their incest, this idea has no basis in fact. Justice Spelman's report of the trials makes no mention of Jane and states that the evidence was provided posthumously by Lady Bridget Wingfield. Lancelot de Carles, in his poem on Anne's life and fall, mentions Elizabeth Browne, Lady Worcester, as being the one who provided evidence of incest.

Apart from imperial ambassador Eustace Chapuys' report that Anne Boleyn confided in Jane about the king's sexual problems and Jane then passed this information on to George, a fact which was then laid before George at his trial, there is no surviving primary source that mentions Jane's involvement in their downfall. According to Lancelot de Carles, George is supposed to have exclaimed bitterly, "On the evidence of this one woman you are willing to believe this great evil of me, and on the basis of her allegations you are deciding my judgement." Although George may have been speaking of his wife, equally he may have been speaking of either Lady Wingfield or Lady Worcester; surely he would have said "on the evidence of my wife" if he was referring to Jane.

Sometime around 4th May 1536, two days after his arrest, George Boleyn's wife, Jane Boleyn, Lady Rochford, sent him a message of comfort via Sir William Kingston, Constable of the Tower of London. There is no record of what she wrote, but Kingston reported that Jane had promised to "humbly [make] suit unto the king's highness" for her husband and that George replied that he wanted to "give her thanks". There is no record of Jane petitioning Thomas Cromwell or Henry VIII, but that doesn't mean that she didn't – various documents were damaged or destroyed in the Ashburnham House fire of 1731. Sir Francis Weston's family fought for his release and the French ambassadors Jean, Sieur de Dinteville, and Antoine de Castelnau, Bishop of Tarbes, had interceded on his behalf, yet he was not pardoned so it is unlikely that Jane's pleas to Cromwell or the king would have been any more effective.

The Boleyn siblings were executed in May 1536, and Jane was left in a precarious financial position. She was forced to write to Thomas Cromwell requesting financial support, and calling herself a "poor desolate widow without comfort". Cromwell reacted by interceding for her with the king. Henry VIII then put pressure on Jane's father-in-law, who increased her allowance to £100. Cromwell also helped Jane by giving her a position in the household of the new queen, Jane Seymour, a position which brought Jane into regular contact with Henry VIII's eldest daughter Mary, who gave Jane gifts of fabric and money for her servants. Jane served Jane Seymour, Anne of Cleves and Catherine Howard as a lady of the bedchamber and is recorded as bearing Princess Mary's train at Jane Seymour's funeral in November 1537. In July 1540, during the king's annulment of his marriage to Anne of Cleves, Jane provided evidence, with Ladies Rutland and Edgecombe, that Anne had confessed to them last midsummer day, of the non-consummation of the marriage, helping Henry VIII get out of the marriage. He then went on to marry Jane's fellow lady, Catherine Howard.

This is when things get weird. Jane may have been innocent when it came down to the fall of the Boleyns, but what on earth happened with Catherine Howard's fall? Why did she become involved in Catherine Howard's adulterous liaisons with Thomas Culpeper? How can we defend her actions in 1541?

Well, I had a discussion with historian Julia Fox, author of *Jane Boleyn: The Infamous Lady Rochford*, about Jane's involvement in Catherine's affair with Thomas Culpeper and Julia said that she had considered various theories but had ruled all of them out bar one. Jane didn't need any money; she had been left well provided for by Thomas Boleyn, so she didn't need any monetary persuasion to help the couple. There is no evidence that she was mad before her imprisonment in the Tower, so it was not madness which drove her recklessly to help the couple betray the king. Julia Fox believes, therefore, that she was persuaded to help Catherine once and that she was then on a slippery slope heading in one direction. She'd done it once, so could not refuse again. We also have to take into account that Thomas Cromwell, the man who had helped her in the past, was dead and gone, so she had nobody to turn to, nobody to confide in and to act as a go-between between her and the king. Jane was on her own with a dreadful secret which could cost her her head, and she didn't know what else to do apart from carrying on helping Catherine and Culpeper. She had already incriminated herself so it got harder and harder to back out, so, instead, she just carried on and ended up digging her own grave.

On 13th November 1541, Chapuys reported that Catherine Howard had been moved to Syon House, formerly Syon Abbey, and that Jane had been taken to the Tower of London. On 3rd December 1541, Chapuys recorded that Jane "on the third day of her imprisonment she went mad" and went on to write of how she had been nursed at Russell House on the Strand, the London residence of Sir John Russell, Lord Admiral, and his wife Anne, under the supervision of the king's own doctors so that she would recover and be "executed as an example". On 9th February 1542, she was taken back to the Tower of London, where she was joined on 10th by Catherine Howard.

A bill of attainder against Catherine Howard and Lady Jane Rochford was introduced into the House of Lords on 21st January 1542 and received royal assent on 11th February. According to this bill, Catherine and Jane were guilty of treason and could be punished without there being any need for a trial. Something else which received royal assent in the House of Lord on 11th February was an act "for due process to be had in high treason in cases of lunacy or madness". This meant that "a person becoming insane after the supposed commission of treason, might be tried; or losing his rational faculties after attainder, might be executed", so even if Lady Rochford didn't recover her faculties she could still be executed. Henry VIII was determined to punish her whatever her state of mind and health. It's quite a thing to do – change the law to kill a mad person. Not one of Henry's nicer moments, if you consider that the law remained until it was repealed in Mary I's reign by the Treason Act of 1554.

So, these women were condemned for high treason without a trial and Jane may even have been mentally unstable. Had she been mentally unstable while serving Catherine and helping her to meet Culpeper or was it her imprisonment and sheer terror as to what was going to happen that sent her over the edge? It's impossible to say.

Jane was executed with her mistress, Catherine Howard, within the confines of the Tower of London on 13th February 1542. Eye-witness merchant Otwell Johnson gave an account of their executions in a letter to his brother:

> "I se the Quene and the Lady Retcheford suffer within the Tower, the day following, whos sowles (I doubt not) be with God, for thay made the moost godly and christyan's end, that ever was hard tell of (I thinke) since the worlds creation; uttering thayer lively faeth in the blode of Christe onely, and with goodly words and stedfast countenances thay desyred all christen people to take regard unto thayer worthy and just punnishment with death for thayer offences, and agenst God hainously from thayer youth upward, in breaking all his commandements, and also agenst the King's royall Majesty very daungeriously: wherfore thay being justly condempned (as thay sayed) by the Lawes of the Realme and Parlement, to dye, required the people (I say) to take example at them, for amendement of thayer ungodly lyves, and gladdly to obey the King in all things, for whos preservation they did hartely pray; and willed all people so to do: commending thayer sowles to God, and ernestly calling for mercy upon him: whom I besieche to geve us grace, with such faeth, hope, and charite at our departing owt of this miserable world, to come to the fruytion of his godhed in joy everlasting."

Edward Hall recorded that they "confessed their offences, and died repentaunt" and Charles Wriothesley simply stated that "the sayd Quene, otherwise Lady Katharine Haward, was beheaded within the Tower on the grene, and my Lady of Rochforde allso; the Lordes of the Counsell, with other noblemen, and certaine commoners, beinge there present at the execution." The eye-witness account and the chroniclers' accounts do not corroborate the claim that Jane Boleyn confessed on the scaffold to her involvement with the fall of her husband, George, and her sister-in-law, the queen:

> "God has permitted me to suffer this shameful doom as punishment for having contributed to my husband's death. I falsely accused him of loving, in an incestuous manner, his sister, Queen Anne Boleyn. For this I deserve to die. But I am guilty of no other crime."

Historian John Guy pointed out that this is from a fictional account, and that the speech is a forgery. He states that this was "the much later work of Gregorio Leti who (says historian Patrick Collinson after investigating many such stories) 'invented some of his sources and made things up'."

The two women were buried in the Chapel of St Peter ad Vincula at the Tower of London.

Notes and Sources

ed. Baker, J.H. (1977) *The Reports of Sir John Spelman*, Selden Society, London, pp. 70-71.

de Carles, Lancelot, "Poème sur la Mort d'Anne Boleyn", lines 861-864, in *La Grande Bretagne devant L'Opinion Française depuis la Guerre de Cent Ans jusqu'a la Fin du XVI Siècle*, Georges Ascoli.

Cherry, Clare, and Ridgway, Claire (2014) *George Boleyn: Tudor Poet, Courtier & Diplomat*, p. 243.

'Henry VIII: May 1536, 16-20', in Letters and Papers, Foreign and Domestic, Henry VIII, Volume 10, January-June 1536, ed. James Gairdner (London, 1887), pp. 371-391. British History Online http://www.british-history.ac.uk/letters-papers-hen8/vol10/pp371-391.

Cavendish, George (1825) *The Life of Cardinal Wolsey*, Volume 2, Samuel Weller Singer, p.220.

Fox, Julia (2008) *Jane Boleyn: The Infamous Lady Rochford*, Phoenix.

Hall, Edward (1809) *Hall's chronicle: containing the history of England, during the reign of Henry the Fourth, and the succeeding monarchs, to the end of the reign of Henry the Eighth, in which are particularly described the manners and customs of those periods. Carefully collated with the editions of 1548 and 1550*, printed for J. Johnson; F.C. and J. Rivington; T. Payne; Wilkie and Robinson; Longman, Hurst, Rees and Orme; Cadell and Davies; and J. Mawman; London. p.843.

Wriothesley, Charles (1875 edition) *A chronicle of England during the reigns of the Tudors, from A.D. 1485 to 1559*, Volume 1, Camden Society, p. 134.

'Spain: December 1541, 1-20', in *Calendar of State Papers, Spain, Volume 6 Part 1, 1538-1542*, ed. Pascual de Gayangos (London, 1890), pp. 406-425. *British History Online* http://www.british-history.ac.uk/cal-state-papers/spain/vol6/no1/pp406-425

'Henry VIII: January 1542, 11-20', in Letters and Papers, Foreign and Domestic, Henry VIII, Volume 17, 1542, ed. James Gairdner and R H Brodie (London, 1900), pp. 10-19. British History Online http://www.british-history.ac.uk/letters-papers-hen8/vol17/pp10-19

ed. Ellis, Henry (1825) *Original letters, illustrative of English history*, Volume II, Harding, Triphook, and Lepard, p.128.

Catherine Howard – Was she really Henry VIII's "rose without a thorn"?

Thank you to Lauryn Poe for inspiring this post and to Conor Byrne, Marilyn Roberts and Judith Loriente for the subsequent discussions on this issue.

Lauryn contacted me to ask whether I knew of a primary source for Henry VIII referring to Catherine Howard as his "rose without a thorn". I was already researching Catherine myself and hadn't come across a source during my research, just historians saying that Henry referred to her as such. I decided to do some digging into it as that's what I like best, a mystery, something to get to the bottom of.

I consulted the secondary sources on my bookshelf. In *The Six Wives of Henry VIII*, Alison Weir wrote that "Henry was so besotted with Katherine that he ordered a medal to be struck in commemoration of their marriage. It was of gold, embossed with Tudor roses and true lovers' knots entwined, and it carried the inscription: HENRICUS VIII: RUTILANS ROSA SINE SPINA, a pretty reference to the King's rose without a thorn, his perfect bride", but there was no reference cited. Fortunately, I had better luck with Antonia Fraser's *The Six Wives of Henry VIII*. In her book, Fraser wrote that "To Henry VIII, Katherine Howard was his 'blushing rose without a thorn'." and in her notes, she gave the Latin motto, RUTILANS ROSA SINE SPINA (blushing rose without a thorn) and cited Agnes Strickland, the Victorian historian, as her source. I have Strickland's *The Lives of the Queens of England*, Volume II, so I checked, and Strickland wrote:

> "He could neither afford to honour Katherine Howard with a public bridal nor a coronation, but he paid her the compliment of causing gold coins to be struck in commemoration of their marriage, bearing the royal arms of England, flanked with H R, and surmounted with the royal diadem. On the reverse is a rose, crowned, in allusion to his bride, flanked by the initials K R, with the following legend:- HENRICUS VIII. RUTILANS ROSA SINE SPINA."

Strickland did not give any more details on the coin struck for Catherine, so I then went digging into Tudor coins. In *Dye's Coin Encyclopaedia*, I found that Henry VIII "introduced the 'Gold Crown' into the English series of coinage" and that this coin had "upon its obverse a double rose, crowned between the letters 'H.R.' (Henry Rex). 'H.A.' (Henry and Anne). 'H.J.' (Henry and Jane). 'H.K.' (Henry and Katherine)". It bore the legend "HENRIC. VIII. RUTILANS ROSA SIE SPIA", or *Henricus VIII., Rutilans rosa sine spina*, meaning "Henry VIII, the shining/dazzling rose without a thorn. So, this encyclopaedia was stating that the legend described Henry, not Catherine.

I then consulted other coin books and websites. In *Coins of England and Great Britain*, Tony Clayton stated that the "Crown of the Rose" coin was "an extremely rare coin struck during the second coinage of Henry VIII for a few months in 1526" and explained that there were "two types, both of which feature a large rose on the reverse. One has the inscription HENRIC RUTILANS ROSA SINE SPINA, meaning 'Henry a dazzling rose without a thorn', and the other DNS HIB RUTILANS

ROSA SINE SPINA, meaning 'Lord of Ireland a dazzling rose without a thorn'." Henry VIII was still married to Catherine of Aragon in 1526, so this coin was not a medal struck in celebration of his marriage to Catherine Howard. Thomas Snelling's *A View of the Silver Coin and Coinage of England from the Norman Conquest* gave the same information as *Dye's Coin Encyclopaedia*. In *Henfrey's Guide to English Coins*, it said:

"Crown. Obv. a double rose crowned, between the letters H.K. (for Henry, and Katherine his 1st wife); or H.A. (for Henry, and Anne his 2nd wife); or H.I. (for Henry, and Jane his 3rd wife); or the letters H.R. (for Henricus Rex). All these letters are crowned. HENRIC VIII. RVTILANS ROSA SIE SPIA."

It also described the half-crown as being similar but with uncrowned letters next to the legend.

On the Portable Antiquities Scheme website, which records archaeological finds, I found a photo of a gold crown from Henry VIII's reign which was dated 1509-1526 and bore a crowned H and R with the legend "HENRIC VIII RUTILANS ROSA SINE SPINA". On the Coin and Bullion Pages website, there are photographs of each side of "the Crown of the Double Rose" which has the crowned initials H and I (I was for Jane, the I and J being used interchangeably at the time) either side of the Tudor rose on one side and Henry VIII's arms on the other. It also bears the legend HENRIC VIII. RVTILANS ROSA SIE SPIA, which is proof that the legend was being used before Henry had even met Catherine Howard.

When I spoke to Conor Byrne, author of *Katherine Howard: A New History*, about my doubts over the coin being struck for Catherine Howard he pointed out that David Starkey had pointed this out in his book on the six wives. "Why hadn't I looked at that book first?", I asked myself. In his notes on his chapter on Catherine, Starkey writes that the motto "originates with Agnes Strickland" and that the coin in question, the Crown of the Double Rose, "had been issued since Wolsey's recoinage of 1536." He went on to explain that after Jane Seymour's death the coin bore the cypher "HR" and remained that way from 1537 until the end of Henry's reign. He also stated, as I'd found out, that the motto/legend referred to Henry. Starkey concluded that the rose badge and motto had nothing to do with Catherine and that "this reading of the evidence is confirmed by M. Siddons, Heraldic Badges of England and Wales. Dr Siddons finds that Catherine, unlike Henry's other wives, seems to have displayed no personal badge." That would explain why the only image of Catherine's rose badge I've been able to find is the one from the Weidenfeld & Nicolson archive, a publisher established in 1948. I have not been able to find any mention of Catherine's "rose" badge in any primary sources or any images of it from historic houses. The badges or "arms" Antonia Fraser writes of being inserted by Galyon Hone, the king's glazier, at Rochester, and quickly removed in 1542 after Catherine's fall, may well have been a cipher like the "HA" ciphers (Henry and Anne) that Henry tried to get removed from Hampton Court Palace after Anne Boleyn's fall. If anyone knows of any badges depicting a rose for Catherine, then please do let me know.

David Starkey writes of how Agnes Strickland's "rose without a thorn" story "has been repeated, with less excuse, by her many successors" and it's true. I am one of those "successors", I have been guilty of writing of Henry VIII referring to Catherine as his "rose without a thorn" and also "a perfect jewel of womanhood", which were his privy council's words and not his own. Henry VIII may well have believed Catherine to be unblemished and perfect, but the romantic motto and badge seem to be fiction. What a shame!

So, we go from Catherine being Henry VIII's "blushing rose without a thorn" to Henry VIII being the "dazzling rose without a thorn", interesting.

Notes and Sources

Weir, Alison (2007) *The Six Wives of Henry VIII*, Vintage, p.436.

Fraser, Antonia (1992) *The Six Wives of Henry VIII*, W&N, pp.405, 437, 548.

Strickland, Agnes (1866) Lives of the Queens of England, Volume II, Longmans Green, Reader and Dyer, pp.351-2.

Dye, John S (1883) *Dye's coin encyclopædia: a complete illustrated history of the coins of the world*, Bradley & Company, p.771.

Clayton, Tony (2013) *Coins of England and Great Britain* ('Coins of the UK') – see http://www.coins-of-the-uk.co.uk/fours. html

Snelling, Thomas (1762) A *View of the Silver Coin and Coinage of England, from the Norman Conquest to the Present Time*, Printed for T. Snelling, p.12.

Henfrey, Henry William (1870) A Guide to the Study and Arrangement of English Coins (Henfrey's Guide to English Coins), John Russell Smith, p.38.

Portable Antiquities Scheme – see http://finds.org.uk/database/artefacts/record/id/449941

Starkey, David (2003) *The Six Wives of Henry VIII*, Harper Collins, p.810 (note 17 to chapter 73).

'Henry VIII: November 1541, 11-20', in Letters and Papers, Foreign and Domestic, Henry VIII, Volume 16, 1540-1541, ed. James Gairdner and R H Brodie (London, 1898), pp. 613-629. British History Online http://www.british-history. ac.uk/letters-papers-hen8/vol16/pp613-629, 12 November 1541, The Council to Paget, Ambassador in France: "The King, on sentence given of the [invalidity] of his marriage with Anne of Cleves, being solicited by his Council to marry again, took to wife Katharine, daughter to the late lord Edmund Howard, thinking [now in his old] age to have obtained [a jewel] for womanhood."

Crown of the Double Rose, http://www.coinandbullionpages. com/english-gold-coins/gold-crown.html.

Lady Jane Grey and Mary I –
Who was the usurper?

Mary I became queen on 19th July 1553 after she successfully deposed her first cousin once removed, Lady Jane Grey, or Queen Jane. Jane had been proclaimed queen following King Edward VI's death on 6th July 1553, having been named as Edward's heir in his "devise for the succession", but her reign was to be only thirteen days. Mary proclaimed herself queen, rallied support and won this game of thrones, imprisoning Jane and eventually executing her on 12th February 1554.

Jane has gone down in history as "Lady Jane Grey" or "the Nine Days Queen", rather than Queen Jane, and is seen as either a tragic victim, a pawn of the Greys and Dudleys, or as a usurper. Mary I hasn't been treated kindly by history, being labelled "Bloody Mary", but her accession is not often seen as usurpation.

How can Mary *not* be a usurper though?

Mary may have been added back into the line of succession after Edward by her father, Henry VIII, along with her half-sister, Elizabeth, in the Third Act of Succession, but this act had not changed the girls' status, they were still illegitimate. When the dying Edward VI came to make arrangements for the succession in 1553, he passed over his half-sisters, making it clear that he viewed them as "clearly disabled" from making any claim to the throne due to their status and the fact that they were "but of the halfe bloud". He chose, instead, to name Lady Jane Grey as his successor, a girl who he deemed to be "whole blood" and his legitimate successor due to her descent from King Henry VII via Mary Tudor.

Hmmm… Henry VIII's Act of Succession versus Edward VI's Devise for the Succession, which one should have taken precedence?

Well, this is always going to be a subject of debate. People often point out that Edward's wishes were not lawful because they went against his father's and because he was still in his minority. However, as Eric Ives pointed out in his book on Lady Jane Grey, Edward VI had the law on his side whereas his father, in adding Edward's half-sisters back into the line of succession, "had interfered with the common law of inheritance". Ives goes on to explain that "Accepting Mary meant setting aside the inheritance rights of legitimate heirs in favour of a bastard. Accepting Jane meant a return to common law. That was the choice. True, Edward was asserting royal prerogative, but in doing so he was restoring the legitimate line of inheritance, and that was what mattered." Common Law, which had been recognised for hundreds of years, ruled that illegitimate children could not inherit, thus protecting the interests of legitimate heirs.

But what about the Third Act of Succession giving the monarch the power to change the succession through his will? Well, if it made it legal for Henry VIII to do so, then it was also legal for his son. Henry could name his daughters as his successors after Edward, but then Edward could name Lady Jane Grey as his successor.

A point made by Beth von Staats, author of *Thomas Cranmer in a Nutshell*, in a discussion a group of us were having on this topic on The Anne Society Facebook page, is that Edward VI was crowned as Supreme Monarch and the powers invested in him at his coronation in February 1547 exceeded those of his father.

He was referred to as "lawmaker", so what Edward stated in his "devise" was law. Edward was the king, and he had named Jane as his successor.

Whatever you think about the morality of it all, what was actually "right", Henry VIII had not taken the step of having his daughters made legitimate once again; he had not protected their interests. I don't believe that Mary and Elizabeth should ever have been made illegitimate. Even though their mothers' marriages to their father had been annulled, they had been conceived in good faith and so should have been recognised as legitimate. However, the law had made them illegitimate, and so this affected their claims. Jane had no such impediment; she was legitimate, and she had Tudor blood.

My own view is that Jane was the rightful queen and should be known as Queen Jane. I see Mary's actions as usurpation, however understandable they were.

Notes and Sources

"Queen Jane or Lady Jane Grey", a talk by Claire Ridgway for the Tudor Society, July 2016.

Ives, Eric (2011) *Lady Jane Grey: A Tudor Mystery*, Wiley-Blackwell.

Third Act of Succession – this can be read at http://www.luminarium.org/encyclopedia/actsuccession3.htm

Thank you to Conor Byrne, James Peacock, Beth von Staats and Catherine Brookes for the discussions on this topic on The Anne Society Facebook page - https://www.facebook.com/SocietyAnne/.

Context is king

This article was inspired by the fact that I had recently been answering lots of emails and comments on social media with a reminder for people to think about the context of the event or person's actions when they were judging that person or coming to a conclusion.

The Oxford Dictionaries website defines "context" as "The circumstances that form the setting for an event, statement, or idea, and in terms of which it can be fully understood." Now when we are discussing Tudor history and Tudor people, we are talking about things that happened and people that lived 400-500 years ago. The world was a very different place then, "the circumstances that form the setting" for these people's lives would be quite alien to us.

How was it different?

Well, that's a huge question, and it's hard to answer without being able to travel back in time. Let's consider just a few differences.

The Tudors were very religious and superstitious. The religious calendar controlled people's daily lives – when they could eat meat, when they could get married or have sexual relations, when they could work or rest, everything. It also affected the way they thought. They believed in original sin and believed that they were all sinners deserving of death, which is why you have people accepting their fates on the scaffold even if they were innocent of the crime with which they had been charged.

Henry VIII was God's anointed sovereign, he had been anointed with holy oil at his coronation and he was the monarch that God wanted to lead England, or so he and his people believed. Accusations are often levelled at Anne Boleyn, with her being branded a home-wrecker, and people often ask how Anne could do what she did to Catherine of Aragon? But, if you put yourself in Anne's shoes, if you consider the context, then you can begin to understand. The King of England chose her. Here was God's anointed sovereign, the man chosen by God to govern England, telling her that his marriage to Catherine was invalid and wrong, and telling her that he wanted her. Anne rebuffed the king for a time, but I expect that he was very persuasive, and what was she supposed to believe or do? I expect that like Catherine Parr in 1543, Anne accepted the king's wishes as her destiny, as her path, as God's will for her.

Although we find it ridiculous that Henry VIII believed that his marriage to Catherine of Aragon was cursed, that God did not bless it because it was against God's law, and it appears to have been a convenient excuse to annul it, it is highly likely that Henry believed this. In Henry's eyes, there must have been a reason for Catherine suffering stillbirths and miscarriages, for little Henry, Duke of Cornwall, dying in infancy: God must not have been happy.

Of course, when Anne produced a girl and then lost two babies it left Henry VIII thinking that God wasn't happy that time round either.

It's hard for us today to understand Henry VIII's obsession with having a son. We live in more enlightened times, we know that women can govern a country just as well as men, but we have to consider context when we look at Henry VIII. England wasn't long out of a time of civil war, decades of struggles and battles caused by two royal houses fighting for the throne, so Henry VIII needed to make the succession secure, and for that, he needed a son, and a spare to be on the safe side. A girl was no good. Women were seen as incapable of ruling, and if a queen married a foreign prince then her husband, and a foreign power, would control the country. Henry VIII had every reason to want and need a son. And don't forget that death was all around. People did not expect to live a long life, and so it was important to secure the future of their family, and in Henry VIII's case the throne.

The Tudors also believed in destiny, fate and omens. Women who were pregnant tried to avoid seeing gruesome sights as it was thought this would affect their unborn child. Eating strawberries while pregnant may cause the baby to have a strawberry birthmark, seeing a hare might cause the baby to have a hare lip… These were superstitious times. No wonder Henry VIII doubted his marriage to Catherine when he was God's anointed king and should have been blessed with children. Dead babies were surely omens, signs that something wasn't right.

Then we have the different views on women, children, childhood and education. I realise that our modern world still has some way to go with regard to equality of the sexes, but the role of women was very different back in Tudor times. Girls were brought up to run a household and to care for children. Men like Thomas More, Thomas Boleyn and Anthony Cooke, who educated their daughters to a high standard, were unusual. A father didn't want to over-educate his daughter as it might put off a husband, it was best to simply give her the skills she needed.

Noble parents would be on the lookout early on for a suitable match for their daughter. Royal and noble betrothals could be conducted with very young children, after all, you wouldn't want to miss out on securing a match between your daughter and the local heir to a fortune, and marriages could take place around the age of 12-14 for girls and 14 for boys. These boys and girls weren't seen as children; they were adults. Children under seven were treated as children, they were innocent and incapable of mortal sin, but after seven they began a more formal education and were treated more like mini-adults. By 12-14 they were marriageable, and if they belonged to the lower classes, then they could start an apprenticeship.

We often think of medieval and Tudor parents as harsh, but they loved their children just like we love ours. As Ralph Houlbrooke points out in his book, *The English Family*, it was believed that spoiling children led to them being physically and morally soft and prone to sickness and vices. It was the parents' responsibility to ensure that their children were not pampered, but instead strictly controlled for the good of their bodies and souls. Affection and love for children were seen as natural and instinctive, but they were not to be lavished on children. Discipline and restraint were the key elements in bringing up children the right way, and many medieval and early Tudor writers urged corporal punishment for correction. Proverbs 13 verse 24 says "He who spares the rod hates his son, but he who loves him is careful to discipline him" and this was taken quite literally. We may think of Tudor parents as abusive; they would see themselves as loving, as doing the best by their children. You didn't strike your child out of hatred or cruelty (well, most parents didn't), you did it out of love. You didn't force your 14-year-old daughter into marriage because you didn't love her, you were making a good match for her and securing her future. An older man didn't marry a much younger woman, a girl even, because he was a paedophile, he was doing something that was normal at that time, he was offering a young girl security, status and wealth in return for children.

As I said earlier in this post, the monarch was God's anointed sovereign, God's chosen leader for the country. That is what the common people believed, and noble families felt that it was their duty to serve that monarch, it was their destiny. There are often comments today on social media about how families were irresponsible or stupid for sending their children to court to serve the king because of the risk of execution or daughters becoming involved romantically with Henry VIII etc., but that's nonsense. It was your duty to serve your king, and it was a great honour for your son or daughter to be appointed to serve the king or his queen. If your child or relative was executed as a traitor, then you grieved in private, picked yourself back up, dusted yourself off and got back to serving God's anointed sovereign as was your duty. You now had to prove your loyalty and that of your family. You had to put your master and king first, and the future security of your family depended on your loyal service to the king. When Thomas Boleyn returned to court after his children's executions, he wasn't heartless, it isn't proof that he didn't love them, that he was overambitious or that he was an awful father, he was doing his duty and doing the best by his surviving family.

Here, I am only scratching the surface. These people lived according to their faith; their routines were controlled by religion, the position of the sun in the sky, the seasons and religious feasts, the farming calendar. Atticus Finch in *To Kill a Mockingbird* tells Scout "You never really understand a person until you consider things from his point of view... until you climb into his skin and walk around in it", and it's so true. We have absolutely no hope of completely understanding the likes of Henry VIII, Thomas Boleyn, Anne Boleyn, or any Tudor person. We cannot climb into their skin, we cannot walk a mile in their shoes, we can never understand their context, the world they lived in, the lives they led, we're just too far removed. And if we cannot understand their world then how can we judge them?

Context is king. Context is everything.

Henry VIII – From Renaissance prince to tyrant

The following article is based on a talk I did for the group on the Discover the Tudors tour in September 2018.

"The heavens laugh, the earth exults, all things are full of milk, of honey and of nectar! Avarice is expelled the country. Liberality scatters wealth with bounteous hand. Our King does not desire gold or gems or precious metals, but virtue, glory, immortality […]"

"[…] a young man who is the everlasting glory of our time […] a king as will wipe the tears from every eye and put joy in the place of our long distress [...]"

"I cannot express the gifts of grace and of nature that God endowed him with all [...]"

"[…] he is so covetous that all the riches in the world would not satisfy him […] he does not reflect that to make himself rich he has impoverished his people, and does not gain in goods what he loses in renown […] he will not cease to dip his hand in blood as long as he doubts his people. Hence every day edicts are published so sanguinary that with a thousand guards one would scarce be safe […] has perverted the rights of religion, marriage, faith and promise, as softened wax can be altered to any form."

These four quotations describe the same man; they describe that iconic Tudor monarch, King Henry VIII.

The first three texts were written by Lord Mountjoy, Sir Thomas More and chronicler Edward Hall on the accession of the seventeen-year-old Henry VIII to the throne in April 1509 following the death of his father, Henry VII. The negative description in the fourth text was written by the French diplomat, Charles de Marillac, resident ambassador at the court of Henry VIII from 1538 to 1543. It was written in August 1540 following the annulment of Henry VIII's marriage to Anne of Cleves, his subsequent marriage to Catherine Howard and the execution of his former right-hand man, Thomas Cromwell.

Thirty-one years separated these comments. In those years, a good-looking, golden-haired, fun-loving, athletic man with all the qualities of the ideal Renaissance prince – intelligence, a lover of the arts, a patron of the arts, a pious man, a poet, musician, composer etc. - had turned into a monster, a tyrant, a man who'd executed many hundreds of people, including his friends and even his wife. He'd broken with Rome; he'd dissolved the monasteries and changed the landscape of England forever, but how and why?

In 1509, those at the royal court and the common people had high hopes for the new king. They had tired of the old king with his unpopular taxation, and this new younger model seemed like a breath of fresh air. On his accession, the Spanish ambassador wrote that "He has released many prisoners and arrested all those responsible for the bribery and tyranny of his father's reign. The people are very happy and few tears are being shed for Henry VII. Instead, people are as joyful as if they had been released from prison."

Lord Mountjoy wrote to the famous humanist scholar, Erasmus:

"I have no fear, my Erasmus, but when you heard that our Prince, now Henry the Eighth, whom we may well call our Octavius, had succeeded to his father's throne, all your melancholy left you at once. For what may you not promise yourself from a Prince, with whose extraordinary and almost divine character you are well acquainted, and to whom you are not only known but intimate, having received from him (as few others have) a letter traced with his own fingers? But when you know what a hero he now shows himself, how wisely he behaves, what a lover he is of justice and goodness, what affection he bears to the learned, I will venture to swear that you will need no wings to make you fly to behold this new and auspicious star.

Oh, my Erasmus, if you could see how all the world here is rejoicing in the possession of so great a Prince, how his life is all their desire, you could not contain your tears for joy. The heavens laugh, the earth exults, all things are full of milk, of honey and of nectar! Avarice is expelled the country. Liberality scatters wealth with bounteous hand. Our King does not desire gold or gems or precious metals, but virtue, glory, immortality [...]"

Ambassador Giustinian said that Henry was "much handsomer than any sovereign in Christendom, a great deal handsomer than the king of France. He was very fair, and his whole frame admirably proportioned... He was very accomplished, and a good musician; composed well; was a capital horseman; and a fine jouster; spoke good French, Latin and Spanish; was very religious, heard three masses a day when he hunted, and sometimes five on other days, besides hearing the office daily in the Queen's chamber, that is to say vespers and compline. He was extremely fond of hunting, and never took that diversion without tiring eight or ten horses, which he caused to be stationed beforehand along the line of country he meant to take. He was also fond of tennis, at which game it was the prettiest thing in the world to see him play, his fair skin glowing through a shirt of the finest texture."

Thomas More praised the new king in verse:

> "This day is the [end] of our slavery, the beginning of
> our freedom, the end of sadness, the source of joy,
> for this day consecrates a young man who is the everlast-
> ing glory of our time and makes him your king-
> a king who is worthy not merely to govern a single
> people but singly to rule the whole world-
> such a king as will wipe the tears from every eye
> and put joy in the place of our long distress.
> Every heart smiles to see its cares dispelled, as the day
> Shines bright when clouds are scattered.
> Now the people, freed, run before their king with bright
> faces. Their joy is almost beyond their own
> comprehension.
> They rejoice, they exult, they leap for joy and celebrate
> their having such a king. "The King" is all that any
> mouth can say."

Polydore Vergil compared Henry to his grandfather Edward IV:

> "For just as Edward was the most warmly thought of by the English people among all English kings, so this successor of his, Henry, was very like him in general appearance, in greatness of mind and generosity and for that reason was the more acclaimed and approved of all."

Chronicler Edward Hall wrote:

> "The features of his body, his goodly personage, his amiable visage, princely countenance, with the noble qualities

of his royal estate, to every man known, needs no rehearsal, considering that, for lack of cunning, I cannot express the gifts of grace and of nature that God endowed him with all."

It's easy to forget this young Henry VIII, the man who saved Catherine of Aragon from an uncertain future and who was devoted to her, the man who loved chivalry and who dressed as Robin Hood to surprise his wife, a generous king, a fun-loving man who enjoyed dancing, who wrote music and verse, who preferred hunting to business, a man who defended Catholicism from the likes of Martin Luther, a generous man who rewarded those around him and who was seen at first as being overly generous. We might complain that Jonathan Rhys Meyers of "The Tudors" series didn't look like our view of Henry VIII, but he certainly did a wonderful job of playing the young, charming, witty and arrogant Henry, a Henry that women could fall in love with, and men could die for. He was seen as a new messiah, a saviour of England. Isn't that a Henry you'd have liked to have known?

But he wasn't all sweetness and light. His father's former loyal advisors, Sir Richard Empson and Sir Edmund Dudley were thrown into prison on the accession of Henry VIII and convicted of treason. Just a year after Henry VIII's accession, they were beheaded. They were used as scapegoats for his father's unpopular system of taxation.

Thomas More may have praised the new king to high heaven in his epigram, "Coronation Ode of King Henry VIII", writing that England's days of slavery were ended, describing Henry as the everlasting glory of our time, but in 1525 he told his son-in-law "if my head would win him a castle in France, it should not fail to go". He later warned Thomas Cromwell "If you will follow my poor advice, you shall, in your counsel-giving unto his grace, ever tell him what he ought to do, but never what he is able to do... For if a lion knew his own strength, hard were it for any man to rule him."

In 1530, the king's former chief advisor, Cardinal Thomas Wolsey, fell from power after failing to get the annulment of the king's marriage to Catherine of Aragon. He died on his journey to London to answer charges of praemunire. Just before he died, Wolsey said to Sir William Kingston, who had been sent to escort him to London:

"He is sure a prince of a royal courage, and hath a princely heart; and rather than he will either miss or want any part of his will or appetite, he will put the loss of one half of his realm in danger. For I assure you I have often kneeled before him in privy chamber on my knees the space of an hour or two to persuade him from his will and appetite; but I could never bring to pass to dissuade him therefrom. Therefore, Master Kingston, if it chance hereafter you to be one of his privy council (as for your wisdom and other qualities ye be meet so to be) warn you to be well advised and assured what matter ye put in his head; for ye shall never pull it out again."

A stark warning.

I believe that Henry became a tyrant. The definitions of "tyrant" that I found are "a cruel and oppressive ruler." and "a ruler who exercises absolute power oppressively or brutally". He did cruel acts, and he was oppressive.

Henry VIII had his wife of over two decades, Catherine of Aragon, a woman who had been nothing but loyal to him, banished from court and separated from her daughter, Mary. Mary was treated cruelly by her father and bullied by his councillors. The imperial ambassador, Eustace Chapuys, feared that she would be executed if she did not submit to her father's will and accept the annulment of her parents' marriage and her father as head of the church.

A young woman, Elizabeth Barton, the Nun of Kent, who spoke out against the annulment but who was probably mentally ill, was executed. Henry VIII broke with Rome and denied the pope's authority, becoming Supreme Head of the Church on England, and in 1535 Sir Thomas More and Bishop John Fisher were executed for treason for refusing to accept the king's supremacy. In the 1530s, the Carthusian monks of London Charterhouse were hanged, drawn and quartered or starved to death for refusing the oath. In 1536, Henry turned on his second wife following her miscarriage, and she was executed, along with men who had served the king loyally, on trumped-up charges. Henry's reaction to the Pilgrimage of Grace rebellion against his religious changes and dissolution of the monasteries was to mislead the rebel leaders, or downright lie to them, and punish the region by executing inhabitants of towns, villages and hamlets, hanging, drawing and quartering them, and ordering the hangings of monks.

Abbeys and monasteries that had stood for centuries and that had provided social care for the common people were closed and destroyed; shrines were desecrated, their wealth went into the royal coffers. Perceived threats, like the elderly Margaret Pole, his eldest daughter's former governess, were brutally executed. Heretics were burned, those who didn't agree with the king were executed as traitors, acts of attainders were increasingly used to get rid of people. Laws were manipulated to suit his purpose; new laws were enacted to punish those who had defied him. For example, he wanted Jane Boleyn, Lady Rochford, executed, so he brought in a law that allowed him to execute those showing signs of lunacy. Faithful servants like Thomas Cromwell were executed, courtiers and councillors were played off against each other, wives were set aside and even executed, wives were threatened, people were tortured illegally... I'm sure you can think of other awful acts done by or ordered by the king.

Henry VIII expected unquestioning loyalty and obedience. John Guy gives an example: "you must be aware", a high-placed friend advised the Cambridge reformer Hugh Latimer when he first came to court in 1530, "that ye contrary not the king. Let him have his sayings; follow him; go with him." If you did that, then you might just survive.

One priest during the Pilgrimage of Grace rebellion described the king as "a tyrant more cruel than Nero, for Nero destroyed but part of Rome, but this tyrant destroyeth this whole realm." In 1539 the Marquis de Aguilar wrote of how Henry was "growing more inhumane and cruel". Philip Melancthon called him "The English Nero". In 1536 Chapuys likened Henry to Theramenes, one of the Thirty Tyrants of Athens. Cardinal Pole wrote in 1536 "During the 27 years he has reigned he has continually plundered them, and if he was liberal in anything, it was certainly not in things making for the common weal. He has robbed every kind of man, made a sport of the nobility, never loved the people, troubled the clergy, and torn like a wild beast the men who were the greatest honor to his kingdom". Charles de Marillac wrote that the bishops in England "make of him not only a King to be obeyed, but an idol to be worshipped" and stated that evils had arisen in the country as a result. That the king "seems tainted, among other vices, with three which in a King may be called plagues" - that he was covetous, that he was distrustful and fearful, and that he suffered with lightness and inconstancy. He concluded: "The subjects take example from the Prince, and the ministers seek only to undo each other to gain credit, and under colour of their master's good each attends to his own. For all the fine words of which they are full, they will act only as necessity and interest compel them."

But where did it all go wrong? Was there a turning point?

Historians like Suzannah Lipscomb and Derek Wilson see 1536 as a key year. His jousting accident was a blow to his pride and masculinity, it reminded him of his mortality and his need for a son and heir, and it took him away from his beloved sport. Then there was Anne Boleyn's fall, the challenge to his masculinity with the Boleyns having apparently mocked his sexual prowess, the death of Henry Fitzroy, the king's only son at this point, the pilgrimage of Grace rebellion - all challenges to his authority which had to be dealt with brutally. But then Anne is gotten rid of, Jane Seymour gives the king a son and dies before he can get bored of her, Mary submits to her father, the rebellion is squashed and the troublemakers removed, Henry wins, his brutality worked.

Then there's the idea that Henry's tyranny, his change, was due to his health problems – bouts of malaria causing paranoia, pain and hassle from leg ulcers, the idea that his jousting accident caused some kind of brain damage and personality change, old age revealing the true personality under the charming exterior, McLeod Syndrome causing paranoia and depression.

Or was Henry following the model of Machiavelli's perfect ruler? He'd been sent a copy of "The Prince" by Lord Morley, and he can be seen to be a Machiavellian prince in that he took steps to eliminate challenging bloodlines and those he perceived as threatening his throne, he cultivated fear, he became more and more greedy, he broke promises when he felt he needed to, he was obsessed with war, he wanted to go down in history and to be famous as a great man, he was a true friend but also a true enemy, and he could appear pious, faithful, humane, honest and religious, but then flit to the opposite when the need arose.

All the views regarding why Henry changed are possible, but I believe that Henry always had that streak of tyranny in him, as is shown by his reign starting with the executions of Empson and Dudley, and then executing Edmund de la Pole, 3rd Duke of Suffolk, in 1513, and Edward Stafford, Duke of Buckingham, in 1521.

I think challenges to his authority made him feel that he needed to be even more brutal, that that was the way of establishing his authority, of being a strong king. He needed to be strong, the Tudor dynasty was fairly new, and England had only just come out of civil war, and until 1537 he didn't have a legitimate male heir. He had to stamp on any challenge.

But I also agree with David Starkey's view that his relationship with Anne Boleyn had a major impact on him as a king and man, that he was changed and warped by their love affair. His passion for Anne, his determination to set Catherine aside and marry Anne, and his need for a male heir led to what Starkey calls a watershed moment, to Henry ruling his people completely. Before, a king had ruled his people's bodies and the pope had ruled their souls, but by breaking with Rome in order to marry Anne, Henry had made himself ruler of his people's bodies and souls. He had unprecedented power. Chapuys stated that Anne had "so perverted him that he does not seem the same man", but it wasn't Anne as such, Anne didn't create the monster, it was what Henry did to be with Anne.

He became master of Church and State, he remade religion, England and the English people, and he became more and more tyrannical. But he saw his tyranny as being right, as serving a higher purpose. He was David beating Goliath. He was destroying false idols and bringing back true religion. John Guy points out that once men like Foxe and Cranmer had convinced him that he really was Christ's deputy that he believed he had a special relationship with God "and saw himself as a patriarch as much as a king." Did he have a God-complex? Did it all go to his head? Was he intent on making a mark on the world, of being notorious? When his health meant that he couldn't be a great warrior king like Henry V, did he have to make up for it in other ways?

I'll leave you with the words of J. J. Scarisbrick from the conclusion to his biography of Henry:

"Henry was a huge, consequential and majestic figure. At least for some, he was everything that a people could wish him to be – a bluff, confident patriot king who was master of his kingdom and feared no one. By the end of his long reign, despite everything, he was indisputably revered, indeed, in some strange way, loved. He had raised monarchy to near-idolatry. He had become the quintessence of Englishry and the focus of swelling national pride. Nothing would ever be quite the same after he had gone.

Yet, for all his power to dazzle, for all the charm and

bonhomie, which he could undoubtedly sometimes show, and for all the affection which he could certainly give and receive, it is difficult to think of any truly generous or selfless action performed by him and difficult not to suppose that, even those who enjoyed his apparently secure esteem, like Jane Seymour or Thomas Cranmer, would not have been thrown aside if it had been expedient to do so, along with the many others who had entwined their lives around his, given him so much, and yet been cast away."

Notes and Sources

Mumby, Frank Arthur (1913) *The Youth of Henry VIII: A Narrative in Contemporary Letters*, Reprint, Forgotten Books, 2013. pp. 126-7.

Hall, Edward (1809) *Hall's chronicle: containing the history of England, during the reign of Henry the Fourth, and the succeeding monarchs, to the end of the reign of Henry the Eighth, in which are particularly described the manners and customs of those periods*, J. Johnson, p. 508.

Starkey, David (2008) *Henry: Virtuous Prince*, Harper Press, p.264.

Correspondencia de Gutierre Gomez de Fuensalida, embajador en Alemania, Flandes é Inglaterra (1496-1509) Publicada por el duque de Berwick y de Alba, conde de Siruela (1907) pp. 515-517.

Lipscomb, Suzannah (2010) *1536: The Year That Changed Henry VIII*, Lion Hudson.

ed. Walker, Greg (2005) Writing Under Tyranny: English Literature and the Henrician Reformation, Oxford University Press.

'Henry VIII: August 1540, 1-10', in Letters and Papers, Foreign and Domestic, Henry VIII, Volume 15, 1540, ed. James Gairdner and R H Brodie (London, 1896), pp. 481-488. British History Online http://www.british-history.ac.uk/letters-papers-hen8/vol15/pp481-488

ed. Sylvester, Richard S. (1976) *The History of King Richard III and Selections from the English and Latin Poems*, Yale University Press.

Guy, John (2014) *Henry VIII* (Penguin Monarchs), Penguin.

Wilson, Derek (2014) *In the Lion's Court: Power, Ambition, and Sudden Death in the Reign of Henry VIII*, St Martin's Press.

Scarisbrick, J.J. (1981) *Henry VIII*, Methuen Publishing.

"An Audience with David Starkey – Henry VIII: The First Brexiteer?", Hever Castle, August 2018.

Interview with Claire Ridgway

To celebrate the fifth birthday of the Tudor Society in 2019, Catherine Brooks, Tudor Society secretary, interviewed Claire. Here is that interview.

Hello Claire! I'm so excited that Tudor Society members are getting this chance to find out a little more about you. To start with, tell us about your life before the Tudors.

Life before the Tudors? Is that even possible?! Ok, I'll be serious… I trained originally as a primary school teacher and taught for a few years before having my children. When my children became school age, and after we had moved to Spain, I started doing freelance writing. I did all sorts of projects – ghost-writing books, copy-editing, product descriptions, web content, blog articles, travel writing… you name it!

The story of how you became so involved in Tudor history is truly unique. Please tell us about it.

I've always loved the Tudors. My very first experience with them was when I did a project at primary school on Henry VIII and his six wives. He was such a larger-than-life character, and I found it amazing that he'd had six wives and had killed two of them. I revisited the subject at A-Level and then again when I studied the Reformation at university. I just couldn't get enough of those Tudors!

But the "truly unique" experience that started me on my present path was a dream I had in January 2009. Like many people around the world at that time, I'd become rather addicted to "The Tudors" series, so that must have sparked off my dream, but I had a very vivid dream about Anne Boleyn's execution. I was present as a member of the crowd, and all I can remember now is my feeling of horror at knowing she was innocent and that there was nothing I could do to stop her execution and to save her. I tried shouting out, but I was so scared that no sound came out. It was horrible. I woke up in quite a state and shook Tim awake. I told him that I needed to start a website called The Anne Boleyn Files and that I needed to share the truth about her. I just knew that that was what I had to do.

People have said to me that I must have been present at Anne's execution in a past life or something, but I believe that it was simply my brain's way of saving me from my present boredom. I'd had a few projects that weren't at all fulfilling and was so fed up of writing about subjects I wasn't interested in. The Anne Boleyn Files stopped me going insane, and it saved my life. Finally, I could spend my days researching and writing about Tudor history. I am so very blessed.

Then, in 2014, I set up the Tudor Society. I had received so many comments and messages from people who wished that they could get to the UK to hear their favourite historians speak and who also subscribed to history magazines and were disappointed that these weren't Tudor focused. "Why don't I connect historians and Tudor history lovers online?" I thought and "Why not produced a Tudor-history focused magazine"? I believe in bringing history to people, so nobody misses out.

You run the hugely successful Anne Boleyn Files website and social media. Tell us more about that and the video series

you are currently running on The Anne Boleyn Files & Tudor Society YouTube channel.

As well as my work for the Tudor Society, I blog about Anne Boleyn on the Anne Boleyn Files website and share my work and the work of others via my social media platforms – Facebook, Twitter and Instagram. I love the Tudor history community on social media. This year, I've been rather busy on YouTube. I wrote and published "On This Day in Tudor History" back in 2012 and have always shared "on this day" events on social media, but this year I'd thought I'd do something different and so committed myself to doing a video a day. I pick one event each day and then talk about that. It's a lot of fun, and I've even managed to get by when I've been under the weather or been away on tours – phew! People seem to be really enjoying the videos. For those who don't like the video format, I also post the audio as podcasts.

You have written so many wonderful books. Once you knew you need to bring some justice to Anne's memory, where did you start?

Thank you! When I was a complete newbie, I started by using secondary sources such as biographies of Anne Boleyn. It was good to get a feel of the current views and theories. Eric Ives' biography of Anne blew my mind; it was so detailed. I then realised that good historians like Eric Ives shared their sources in the notes sections of their books and their bibliographies. When my friend Clare Cherry informed me that a lot of archives had been digitised, I got so excited. I spent whole days lost in Letters & Papers, reading ambassadors' dispatches, reading contemporary chronicles, lists of grants and expenses, letters…. It was so very exciting. Finding contemporary sources allowed me to interpret things myself and to come to my own conclusions, and these I shared on the Anne Boleyn Files.

Then, in early 2012, my friend Linda, a wonderful lady who I'd come to know through my Anne Boleyn Experience

Tour and the Anne Boleyn Files, told me that I should publish the most popular blog articles from the Anne Boleyn Files as a book. I did this in February 2012, the third anniversary of the Anne Boleyn Files, and the rest is history, as they say. It became a bestseller.

How do you go about researching your work? It can be very tricky to locate and then interpret historical source material.

It's actually not as tricky as it sounds, and it's something I enjoy teaching others. The notes sections and bibliographies of good secondary sources can lead you on a voyage of discovery. Simply google the names of the primary sources, and you will generally find them. My two favourite websites for primary sources are British History Online - https://www.british-history.ac.uk/ - and Archive.org - https://archive.org/. British History Online has so many digitised documents, and Archive has old and out of copyright books, including the contemporary chronicles of Charles Wriothesley and Edward Hall. Wonderful resources for researchers and historians. You can also find things on Google Books.

Interpreting these sources is a little harder, especially if the spelling is a bit dodgy. I read Tudor works out loud in a Captain Jack Sparrow accent, and that helps me to understand it. Then, it might take a while longer, a bit of thinking and a consideration of other historians' views on the document for me to come to my own conclusion.

Your passion for the Boleyns soon extended beyond Anne herself. Popular fiction can occasionally run the risk of perpetuating the common falsehoods that circulate around historical figures. Have you found the Boleyns to be a good example of this?

Yes, I fell in love with the whole Boleyn family! Fiction

and some lazy historians have perpetuated the myths and made members of the Boleyn family caricatures really. We have overly ambitious pimp Thomas Boleyn married to the cold and unfeeling Elizabeth Howard; Mary Boleyn is either a bit flighty and romantic, a woman who chooses love over ambition, or she's Henry VIII's true love; Anne is spitefully ambitious, a social climber and homewrecker who has Henry VIII in some sexual stranglehold and aims for the crown at any cost, and George is homosexual (and this is always presented negatively) and a wife-beater who has a terribly unhappy marriage. There are some days when I feel like I should be wearing armour as I battle against the views that some people hold. It can be very frustrating and tiring to challenge long-held views and perceptions.

Over the years, you have been on a number of Tudor travels. What have been your most memorable trips and which are your favourite places?

Tim and I started doing Tudor history tours in 2010 and did this until 2012, running the Anne Boleyn Experience tour and the Executed Queens tour. However, we became far too busy with other projects and family life so abandoned the idea. But then a friendship with Philippa Lacey Brewell of British History Tours led to us resurrecting the idea and joint-venturing with her. It has worked so well. Last year, we did the Anne Boleyn Experience and the Discover the Tudors Tour, this year we've done the Anne Boleyn Experience and Executed Queens tour, and in 2020 we're doing the Anne Boleyn Experience, Elizabeth I Experience, and Tudor & Stuart Witchcraft & Medicine.

I love these tours. I get to see some stunning places with fellow Tudor history lovers AND get to talk Tudor all the time! Plus, I'm doing it with one of my best mates, Philippa, and we have such fun together. We designed these tours to be "experiences" rather than tours and that's really happening. It's also lovely to see true life-long friendships being made and people coming back again and again.

My most memorable trip? I really can't say. Perhaps this year's Anne Boleyn Experience when we did the Hidden Hever tour for the first time, and then I stayed in the area after the tour and got to hold Anne Boleyn's books of hours. That was a real "pinch me" moment! Hever feels like my second home, I can never get enough of it, so a few days there on the Anne Boleyn Experience is perfect. I get to see my lovely friend Owen, Castle Supervisor, when I'm there too, and the Hever staff are just fabulous.

If an overseas Tudor history lover was to come to the U.K. and could visit only three places, where would you suggest and why? That's a tough one!

That is a tough one, and I'm completely biased! Hever Castle, just because it is so intimate, plus the gardens are breathtaking. If you love Anne Boleyn, you get a real sense of her and her family there, and it's amazing to see the books that she wrote in and that belonged to her.

I love Kenilworth Castle too. I'm a soppy romantic, and I get choked up when I visit there because I think of all the work Robert Dudley did there to try and woo Elizabeth, as a last-ditch attempt to make her marry him.

Then I'm torn between Hampton Court Palace, the Tower of London and Penshurst Place. Sorry, I'm not good at making decisions! HCP is huge and beautiful and has so much history; the Tower has served as a royal palace, a fortress, a mint, a prison, a place of execution.... History is just flowing out of its walls! Then Penshurst is just one of those beautiful properties with lots of portraits, lovely gardens and knowledgeable staff. We had a lovely day there.

Tell us more about your books – of which there are many! Obviously, you began with your work on Anne, but what path did you follow from there?

Ha! Yes! Lots of books. Anne is my first love, and I've written two collections of articles – *The Anne Boleyn Collection* and *The Anne Boleyn Collection II*. I'm getting ready to release *The Anne Boleyn Collection III* at the moment. I was blessed to get to know Clare Cherry through the Anne Boleyn Files, and I thoroughly enjoyed working with her on *George Boleyn*. Clare had done so much research and had actually written a manuscript, but then we wove in my research on Thomas and Elizabeth Boleyn, Anne Boleyn, Jane Boleyn, and the Boleyn's religious views. It was such a fun project, and I'm proud of what we did. It's good to have played a part in rehabilitating George.

On This Day in Tudor History grew out of me sharing "on this day" posts and was a huge project. Obviously, everyone knows key Tudor events, but I wanted to share more obscure events. It took a lot of research, but my readers really enjoyed it, and now it's reaching new people through my videos.

Illustrated Kings and Queens of England was a bit of a family project. I loved Cassell's very old illustrated history and thought it would be good to have a modern book giving brief bios of the kings and queens along with coloured versions of Cassell's illustrations, and a few others. I did the writing and Tim and our daughter Verity did the colour work on the engravings.

I've also done a short book on sweating sickness – a very odd illness! - and a book on Tudor properties and places: *Tudor Places of Great Britain*.

My very favourite project, though, was *The Fall of Anne Boleyn: A Countdown*. I had done a countdown of blog articles, sharing the events which led to Anne's execution in May 1536, but I did more extensive research for the book. Writing it just brought home to me how fast everything happened in 1536 and what an awful miscarriage of justice it had been. It had a real impact on me.

If it's not a secret, can you tell us if you have any writing projects on the go at the moment? It must be a challenge, as you already do so much!

It is a challenge, and one project has been on the backburner since 2012. That project is *The Fall of Catherine Howard: A Countdown*. I really must finish it! The research is pretty much done, and I've created the timeline, I just need to get the book written! I'll get there. As I said, I'm also putting the finishing touches to *The Anne Boleyn Collection III*, and then I'm starting a new project, a joint project with my friend Owen Emmerson, Castle Supervisor at Hever Castle. Our book will be a social history of the castle, introducing the people and families who owned it, as well as the castle they knew. I'm looking forward to properly starting it.

I also have a few more ideas, another project with Owen, but I need to focus on these for now.

Your books, and many others, are published through MadeGlobal Publishing, a company set up by you and your husband, Tim. What have you learned from this as an author?

It's been such a learning curve! I chose to self-publish, i.e. use Tim's skills to publish me, rather than go with traditional publishing because I was quite disillusioned with the publishing world and what I was hearing from other authors. I knew nobody would be interested in publishing a collection of blog articles anyway, so we just did it ourselves. It was good to be in control and to actually make some money from it! The success of that book then led to offers from publishers, but the limited print runs, low royalties, lack of control etc. just put me off. MadeGlobal Publishing was born when authors I had got to know asked about how we did it. We could offer better royalties, a more fair arrangement, so we ended up with quite a few authors on board. As I say, it's been a learning curve, but we've made some good friends along the way and learned a lot. I'm proud of what Tim has achieved and the way he has helped people to get their "baby" out there for readers.

I shall make the question I usually save until last, my penultimate one today: If you could recommend three 'must read' history books, from any period, what would they be?

Ooooh! Tough one! Eric Ives' *The Life and Death of Anne Boleyn*, Gareth Russell's *Young and Fair and Damned*, and Leanda de Lisle's *The Sisters Who Would be Queen*. And because I'm me and I don't stick to rules, I'll add a fourth! "God's Traitors" by Jessie Childs.

Over the years, your writing, websites, social media, and MadeGlobal have brought together authors, researchers, bloggers, and readers from across the world. How does it feel to know that your vision for a fair hearing for Anne Boleyn has forged so many relationships?

Aaaaggghhh, you've made me go all weepy now! I feel so blessed to have these beautiful people in my life.. Most of my present best friends are people I met on this incredible journey, people who have offered me support and encouragement when I've felt like giving up, and I know I do the same for them. I'm a people person, I just love talking Tudor, listening to people, and engaging with my readers too. I feel incredibly privileged to have a platform where I can share information, receive feedback on it straight away, and just chat with people. And it's just amazing when you hear that people enjoy your work, or they admit that they've changed their views because of something you wrote. I love it.

Claire Ridgway is the author of the best-selling books: *George Boleyn: Tudor Poet, Courtier and Dipomat* (co-written with Clare Cherry), *On This Day in Tudor History, The Fall of Anne Boleyn: A Countdown, The Anne Boleyn Collection* and *The Anne Boleyn Collection II, Sweating Sickness in a Nutshell, Tudor Places of Great Britain, Illustrated Kings and Queen of England* and *The Life of Anne Boleyn Colouring Book.*

Claire is the historical oracle (her best friend called her that so she's going with it) behind The Anne Boleyn Files history website, which is known for its historical accuracy. Claire's mission is to get to the truth behind Anne Boleyn's story and to share that with everyone. Claire is also the founder of the Tudor Society, an online hub connecting Tudor history lovers, historians and authors from all over the world, and the woman behind the popular Anne Boleyn Files and Tudor Society YouTube Channel. She also co-leads Tudor history tours with Philippa Lacey Brewell of British History Tours - you could say that Claire is a bit of a Tudor nut!

Acknowledgements

The articles and talks featured in this book would never have seen the light of day if it wasn't for the ongoing support and encouragement of the following people:

Tim Ridgway, Frank and Davida Brassington (Mum and Dad!), Gareth Russell, Owen Emmerson, Alison Palmer, the staff at Hever Castle, Philippa Lacey Brewell, Clare Cherry, Bandit Queen, Mike, Christine and Globerose, Carla Smith, Dawn Hatswell, Lorna Wanstall, British History Tours tour participants, James Peacock, Adrienne Dillard, Sandra Vasoli, Beth von Staats, Catherine Brooks, Tara Ball, Ana Martínez Martínez, Graham Scott, Anna Maria Hayward, Dave & Lou Nelson, and my YouTube channel subscribers.

I am so blessed!

Thank you also to Dmitry Yakhovsky for his beautiful image of Anne Boleyn used on the cover of this book.

Other books by Claire Ridgway

The Anne Boleyn Collection:
The Real Truth About the Tudors

The Anne Boleyn Collection II:
Anne Boleyn and the Boleyn Family

The Anne Boleyn Collection III:
Celebrating Ten Years of TheAnneBoleynFiles

The Fall of Anne Boleyn:
A Countdown

George Boleyn:
Tudor Poet, Courtier & Diplomat (with Clare Cherry)

Illustrated Kings and Queens of England

Tudor Places of Great Britain

Sweating Sickness: In a Nutshell

On this Day in Tudor History

The Life of Anne Boleyn Colouring Book

Made in the USA
Middletown, DE
19 June 2020